The Stone Circle Poems

The Stone

The Collected Poems of Terry Wooten

Parkhurst Brothers Publishers

MARION, MICHIGAN

Circle Poems

www.parkhurstbrothers.com

Parkhurst Brothers books are distributed to the trade through the Chicago Distribution Center, and may be ordered through Ingram Book Company, Baker & Taylor, Follett Library Resources and other book industry wholesalers. To order from Chicago Distribution Center, phone 800-621-2736 or send a fax to 800-621-8476. Copies of this and other Parkhurst Brothers, Inc., Publishers titles are available to organizations and corporations for purchase in quantity by contacting Special Sales Department at our home office location, listed on our website. Manuscript submission guidelines for this publishing company are available at our website.

Printed in the United States of America

First Edition, March 2015

2015 2016 2017 2018   16 15 14 13 12 11 10 9 8 7 6 5 4 3 2 1

Library of Congress Cataloging in Publication Data has been applied for and will appear in this space for future editions.

ISBN: Trade Paperback   978162491-053-1
ISBN: e-book   978162491-054-8

Cover photos and title page photo by	Alan Newton
Page design by	Susan Harring
Cover design by	Linda D. Parkhurst, Ph.D.
Proofread by	Barbara and Bill Paddack
Acquired for Parkhurst Brothers Publishers by	Ted Parkhurst

All photos not credited were provided by the Wooten family.

Believing that a free and open exchange of ideas is essential to the survival of a free people, Parkhurst Brothers Publishers supports the First Amendment of the United States Constitution and encourages readers to study all viewpoints of public policy deliberations.

032015

Dedicated
to

Wendi

Who has been at my side through a lot of thin
and the occasional bit of thick.

Acknowledgements

Looking back over four and a half decades I'd like to thank a few people who assisted or influenced me the most in my journey as a poet. The first has to be my eighth and ninth grade Language Arts teacher Sonya Titus. She set the creative spark in my mind ablaze.

Another person who helped support my creative path was the construction company boss I worked for in Kalamazoo, after I left college to study on my own. Tom Thatcher was the closest thing I ever had to a big brother.

Tom allowed me to work only three days a week, so I had plenty of time to spend on poetry. He also helped secured lodging for me in an attic apartment for $40 a month, when the going rate was four times that much. Tom was my personal living, breathing literary arts grant, and good friend.

Two Western Michigan University college professors, John Cooley and Herb Scott, had major influences on me. The first, John Cooley, I actually had for a writing class. After I left college John and his wife Barb invited me over to their house many times for literary events and conversation. John always had time to comment on my latest collection of poems.

I never attended any of Herb Scott's poetry classes, but he took an interest in my work, especially a series of prose poems I wrote titled *Locust Street Laundromat*. Herb invited me back to the university to read, and taught the collection for years to his students. As one of the editors of the 1988 edition of *Contemporary Michigan Poetry – Poems From The Third Coast*, Herb Scott was the reason I was included in the anthology.

The best and most trusted writer friend I've ever had is Patrick Pfister. In the early years of our friendship we spent many nights in my Locust Street apartment talking shop. After our lives separated we stayed in touch with letters for 40 years. I saved all of his, and have a dresser drawer full. Recently on a visit to our home Patrick gave me bound copies of all of mine. Nobody, except my wife, knows my writing better and has commented on it more than Patrick.

The luckiest Saturday night of my life was meeting my wife at a dance club, and asking her if she wanted to dance the whole next set. Forty years later we joke about how we're still dancing. She's the mother of our children, my agent, business brains, literary critic and best friend. Without her family's support there would be no Stone Circle, and I wouldn't be where I am today.

No list of major influences in my life could be written without mentioning poets Taelen Thomas and Max Ellison. These two men changed the direction of my art, which made it possible for me to eventually make a living reciting my poetry.

A very special thanks to Alan Newton for the beautiful photography on the front cover and title page of this book. Alan's world class photography is matched only by the generosity of his heart.

Last, I want to thank oral historian Glenn Ruggles. Glenn helped me understand the importance of the poet in the community, and to collect the people's stories. Without his guidance there would be no Elders Project.

Terry Wooten
Stone Circle
January, 2015

Notes on Permissions

"Crow Dance," "Story of Kewadin," "Willie," and "Last Words of Max Ellison" were included in *Contemporary Michigan Poetry – Poems From The Third Coast* published by Wayne State University Press, 1988.

The Max Ellison poems were originally published in a chapbook titled *Words Wild with Bloom* by Stone Circle Press.

"Ode to Ernie Harwell" was featured by the *Detroit Free Press*, the *Traverse City Record Eagle* and *The Marion Press*.

"Troublemaker" appeared in *Voices of Michigan* published by Mackinac Jane's Publishing Company, and the *Northern Express*.

"Coyote's Back" appeared in *The Saginaw News*.

Poems from the *Lifelines* and *Child of War* sections of this book were first published in collections with the same titles by The Wordsmith Press.

"Motion" appeared in a collection *A Book of Hours*.

The Elders Poems "Martin Marauders," "Zig Zag," "Loose in London," Iwo Jima 'Beach Party'," "Peace," "Bingo," "Changes," "Halloween," "It Was Him," "The Letter," "Road Art," and "Epiphany" were first published by the Elk Rapids Area Historical Society under the title *Water Under the Bridge*.

"A Rose Red Dress 1926 – 1962," "In Her Arms," and "First Words" appeared in various editions of *Peninsula Writers*.

"Most of these poems were originally published by Stone Circle Press in chapbooks *Okeh, The Stone Circle Anthology, Boulders in Exile, The Stone Circle Anthology II, The Abstracts of Romance, Turn Here,* and *Black and White Cows in the Pasture Paused to Watch*.

Quite a few of the poems in this collection have been featured by the *Traverse City Record Eagle* in my *Lifelines* column, and *The Marion Press*.

The poet's first day of school at Marion Public Schools,
Marion, Michigan, 1953.

Contents

Part One, There was a child went forth – Walt Whitman

Part Two, *But the beauty is not the madness* - Ezra Pound

Part Three, *A lover gambles everything* - Rumi

Part Four, *Old Bob's been dead for forty years,*
But his apple trees still bloom. - Max Ellison

Part Five, Fire is an old story – Gary Snyder

Part Six, Lifelines

Part Seven, Child of War

Part Eight, The Elders Project

A rock is reserved for V.I.P. seating at Stone Circle.

The Fire Begins

A poet-friend, Taelen Thomas, guided my wife, Wendi, and me down a narrow, sandy two-track road a mile through the woods. He insisted we park our car and walk the last 200 yards.

Taelen was taking us to a place called Frog Holler; a natural, acoustic, cathedral-like meadow located in the middle of a wooded valley in Northern Lower Michigan. In the center was a little campfire. He wanted to introduce us to two unique men who had been hobos during their teens in the early 1930s.

One was the unofficial poet laureate of Northern Michigan, Max Ellison. The other, Chuck Shinn, was a philosopher and participant in the sit-down strikes in Flint, Michigan, during the Great Depression. I was a bit nervous. I'd never met real hobos before.

When I was a young boy growing up in Marion, Michigan, Grandpa Wooten told me stories about working on the railroad for a short time. He said hobos would come into their camps at night, and regale the workers with tales of their travels. In return they'd receive a cup of stew or plate of food. Grandpa said some of these hobos were actually quite famous.

The old Ann Arbor Railroad passed by a quarter mile from my mom's parents' home. Grandpa and Grandma Helmboldt lived in a ghost town called Park Lake, located between Marion and another little farming village, McBain. When I was visiting Park Lake and heard the train whistle blow from a few miles through the woods, I'd drop everything and run down a narrow road to watch the freight trains go by. Once, standing there I saw what I'm sure was a hobo. He was standing in an open freight car door, and he waved at me. After hearing Grandpa Wooten's stories, that was big stuff. I ran all the way back to Grandma's house yelling, "I saw a hobo! I saw a hobo!"

Walking the last 200 yards into Frog Holler, I didn't know this short pilgrimage would change my life. Frog Holler was a gathering of people who came and listened to Max share his poetry and poems of others. Near the end of the evening, members of the audience would be invited to enter Max's small house in the woods. In there they could buy his books of poetry and small watercolor paintings and sign his walls. That was his guest book, his white plasterboard walls. I'd never experienced anyplace like it, and was smitten.

It was Saturday of Labor Day weekend 1980. Wendi and I had been married for almost five years, and she'd given birth to our first child four months earlier. We named him Ezra, after one of my favorite poets, Ezra Pound, in honor of Pound's poetry, not his politics. Unfortunately, our son also had the great poet's temper. Ezra was born the same week as the volcano Mount St. Helen erupted, and like the volcano he was always blowing his top. We loved him more than ourselves, but he was a difficult baby.

On September 20, 1975, I'd married into a family of cherry farmers. Farmers are very practical people. You can imagine how thrilled they were when their beautiful, dark-eyed, youngest daughter brought home a poet to meet her parents. When my wife was a little girl, her older siblings always told her she was found on the front porch one morning. It's not true, but I like the story. It's a good myth about why she's a bit different from the rest of the family.

Helping Wendi take care of our newborn son and working on her family's farm, my writing had slowed down, and so had our social life. In this culture of ours there's not a lot for a young couple with a baby to do.

By 1980 I'd been writing poetry for fifteen years, but my art was still sputtering along. While attending college I'd rejected the academic path of teaching and writing poetry. It didn't work for me. A lot of the contemporary poems I read seemed unnecessarily complicated and out of touch with the world outside of academia. I wasn't interested in writing like that, or couldn't. I didn't know what kind of poet I was yet, but I was working hard trying to figure it out. I knew I wanted to write poems in the vernacular of everyday people, and to do that I set out on my own.

I left college and rented a little attic apartment in Kalamazoo, Michigan, which became my home for the next six years. I worked construction during the summers and studied the way people talked. I shelved books at the Western Michigan University library during the winters. I checked out books and studied poets from Chaucer to Whitman. I educated myself.

During this time the Vietnam War was raging, mangling both the Vietnamese people and young American men who got sucked into it. I was a poor white boy and was drafted three times. I stood up against the war, but never the soldiers who fought it. I thought it was an immoral war, and based my stand on Thoreau's essay "Civil Disobedience"; in short, if you think the people in power are doing wrong, rebel, but always behave more civilly than the people you are rebelling against. It's a long story I don't care to get into here. After four years and a meeting with an FBI agent I was given a deferment.

Max Ellison and Taelen Thomas both recited their poetry from memory. Being slightly dyslexic, I couldn't read out loud very well, but I'd never thought about memorizing and reciting my poems, until I met them. Taelen and I were closer in age and in our approaches to poetry, but Max influenced me more – I think because of our similar backgrounds growing up in rural Michigan in small-town farming communities and our working-class ethics.

The location of Frog Holler had once been the grounds of Pleasant Valley Schoolhouse. Max had attended the one-room school as a boy. Now his small twelve-by-sixteen-foot home stood on the old foundation of the school's woodshed. If you looked closely, you could still see the school building's crumbling stone foundation disappearing under sixty years of forest growth. One old photo of this place shows kids perched all over the building. The grown-ups called the place Pleasant Valley, but the kids called it Frog Holler, because of the pond close by.

I came out of my attic incubation steeped in the minimalism of the imagist movement, admiring poets like William Carlos Williams, Ezra Pound and, later, Gary Snyder. Their message, in short, was to write with as few words as possible and with no rhyme.

Max was a pioneer of performing poetry and stories in schools from kindergarten through high schools. He was doing this good work before anyone else that I know of. Meeting him helped me find the last piece of my puzzle as a poet, though our writing styles were different. Max taught me a powerful lesson: that you could make a living as a poet outside of the universities. I knew right away I wanted to do what he was doing, and within a week I had memorized a dozen of my poems. I've been memorizing ever since, and now have more than 570 poems in my repertoire.

I worked with Max Ellison off and on for three years. During this time Wendi and I moved into a bigger house with a four-acre meadow for a backyard. I'd been given a gift by invisible helping hands. Memorization came easy for me. I now had a voice, and entered a strong creative period.

Influenced by Frog Holler and by Gary Snyder's vision of a poet in a more primitive sense, a sort of cultural adhesive that helps holds a community together with its stories, I started building my own poetry forum, which I called Stone Circle. Over the years Wendi's family farm had accumulated a large collection of huge boulders that had been dragged by horses and later bulldozed out of fields. They sat scattered around randomly in stone piles or along old fence lines.

Using the farm's two orchard tractors, I hauled three-billion-year old boulders home to the meadow south of our house. Over the next three years I placed 88 large stones in three concentric circles surrounding a place for a fire in the center. As Gary Snyder wrote, "Fire is an old story." The goal was to create a unique outdoor poetry setting where words were the focus, and poetry a recipe for communication.

Frog Holler was winding down and Max was getting tired. I can't remember how the shift actually happened, but one of us suggested we transfer his poetry gatherings to Stone Circle. For the opening night we held a potluck dinner and were given lots of media coverage by local newspapers.

Two months earlier Wendi had given birth to our second child, a girl. We named her after an Oglala Sioux artist and peace man, Ahbleza, who was said to ride into battle with nothing but a song. Ahbleza means "observer" or "see with his heart." But we softened the spelling to Ablaisia, or Blaise for short. She was a mellower baby than Ezra, but all babies are a lot of work. I began the first Stone Circle gathering holding Blaise on my lap, while Ezra perched nearby listening. With two little kids, a lot of people thought we were taking on way more than we could handle, but our social life certainly wasn't lacking anymore. That first night there were at least 100 people in attendance. We ran every Saturday night until Labor Day weekend with good crowds.

Max was with us at Stone Circle for only one year. The following winter he was diagnosed with an inoperable brain tumor, and died late that spring at 71. So here I was, a fledgling performance poet and father of two young children, host to an outdoor poetry venue that would become an institution. With the help of Taelen Thomas and the wise guidance of Chuck Shinn, I grew into the role. Whereas Frog Holler had pretty much been a one-man show, I tried to steer Stone Circle into more of an open forum for poets who wanted to participate. The word got around.

While building Stone Circle, my vision was to take poetry back to its roots, to create an ambiance reminiscent of when ancient cultures had gathered to celebrate their experiences in poems, songs and stories. I wanted a family event with two rules: the poems should be said by heart, and watch the language if there are children in the audience.

Wendi had taken over the job as Max's booking agent for the last two years of his career. After he passed away we had to decide whether to let the school contacts unravel, or have me take it over. I chose to try to make a living performing poems in schools. It took a couple years of balancing farm work with poetry work, but gradually my bookings in schools and conferences became a full-time job.

During the second year of Stone Circle, I met another individual, Glenn Ruggles, who would have a major influence on my art. Glenn was a writer, an oral historian and a leading member of the Michigan Oral History Association. When he was thirteen, Glenn had moved with his family from the Detroit area up to Elk Rapids. After his initial homesickness and anger about having to leave his old friends behind, he fell in love with the rural community, and its people changed his life. He grew from a rebellious student who was constantly skipping school, to a young man enamored by education.

Now in his 50s and teaching history at a downstate high school, Glenn was visiting the Elk Rapids area regularly and compiling oral history interviews of local people. I'd never met a person with such a passion for oral histories. His troublesome youth had also created a warm spot in his heart for difficult students. Maybe that's what drew him to me, the way I'm drawn to the same type of kid.

Voices on the Water would become one of Glenn Ruggles' master works and his big thank you to the chain of lakes and its characters. I was included in this oral history, though I hadn't lived here nearly as long as any of the other people interviewed. For a long time I felt out of place in the book, but Glenn insisted that I belonged. He shared my vision of a poet being an important part of a community, a person who collects all those stories and various voices.

Glenn loved the Stone Circle and attended quite a few of the early gatherings. He took me under his wing, and managed to get me invited to the MOHA fall conference as a presenter reciting my poetry. Through Glenn's influence I became even more sensitive to people's voices and the conversations going on around me. I fine-tuned the idea that there were lines of poems or material for entire poems being said around us all the time, and that it was the poet's job to be aware of this muse.

Further Along

By 1984 schools were beginning to request writing workshops along with my poetry presentations, so I developed a workshop that mirrored what I did as a writer. To help students find an idea to write about, I have them draw what I call a "Memory Map." It is a simple picture of where they live, used to live or grew up. On the map they mark out various memories that come to mind while they are drawing.

In my "Talking to Write" workshop I use my own memory map or sketch of my hometown as a visual guide to help students to draw their own maps. The location for most of my early poems in this collection could be marked on this sketch. I hadn't lived in Marion, Michigan, for a long time, but those first eighteen years were a formative period. It shows how alive my childhood was.

Mom said I was a curious kid and asked more questions than all three of my younger sisters put together. Looking back it seems I was born a poet, but didn't realize it until eighth grade. Then I kept my interest in writing poetry a secret, because I didn't think football players were supposed to write poetry.

As a teenager I thought my goal in life was be a professional football player, but a little voice kept telling me "that's not it." I was a middle linebacker on defense, and made all-state as a pulling right guard on offense. That's as far as I got. Luckily I didn't grow big enough, and messed up my Scholastic Aptitude Test. When I showed up at college as a walk-on, I was ineligible for two weeks until I retook my SAT's.

I was also harassed by a coach about my long, shaggy hair, "Is that a bird's nest on top of your head?" The fall of 1967 was a very different time. Obviously, the guardian angels or "helping hands" as Joseph Campbell called them, were looking out for me and had better plans. I gave up football and became a long-haired poet. Now I'm a balding, well-known poet with a famous Stone Circle in the meadow behind our home. The circle has become a part of us. My path has been a long journey like a labyrinth. Let's turn around back towards the beginning.

I have two early memories that amount to something. One is meeting a painted turtle while I was morel mushroom hunting with my mother and her sister. I was three and thought it was a rock that had come alive. I peeked into an opening in the shell, and came face to face with a scowling little animal looking back at me. If I had a spirit name it would be "Scowling Turtle."

The other first memory is of my parents fighting and my dad storming out the front door. I followed after him crying. I can still hear mom yelling after me to get back in the house. I grabbed dad's leg and begged him to come back in with me. He did, but divorce was always a looming threat. There are a lot of good memories of my parents, too. Unfortunately, we tend to remember the best and the worst.

I've developed a simple motto over the years. If an experience doesn't destroy you, it can become a gift. One of my most hard-earned gifts was growing up in a loving but troubled family. It has enabled me to connect intuitively with kids who also come from homes where love and dysfunction go hand-in-hand. My high school football experience also helps me reach a certain kind of student who otherwise might think he or she doesn't like poetry.

I spent a lot of time scowling through the early grades in school. Since I was such a curious child, and two of my three sisters came along soon after me, I was put into kindergarten at four years old. Being one of the youngest in my class, and dyslexic, having an inquisitive mind, a wild imagination, and dysfunctional home life all worked against me. I thought I was dumb.

At six years old I experienced a powerful epiphany or vision. I was running down the driveway to get on the school bus. As I passed a mud puddle, I thought, "This is right now. When I run back by here this afternoon is in the future. But when it happens ... it will be right now." Seven hours later I jumped off the bus, ran towards the house, and passed the same puddle. Whoa! Wow! The future happened in the present, and so did the past. A few nights later I was lying in bed waiting for sleep. Alone in the dark I thought, "Someday, hopefully a far time in the future I'm going to grow old and die. When it happens it will be right now."

Terry Wooten in cowboy attire, about age six.

Next morning mom found me curled up in the fetal position, whimpering behind the living room stove. "Now what's wrong?" she asked. I was always wondering or worrying about something. "I don't want to be a skeleton," I whined. One of the reasons I write is to capture those now moments of my life that stand out, so they will still be here in poems after I'm gone. The early poems in this collection show a boy and a young man extremely aware of what's going on around him.

In the 1950s teachers were not trained to identify students like me. Mom saved all my report cards up through sixth grade. I own them now. They're sad to read. A similar thread of teacher comments weaves through the grades: "Terry likes to visit during work time. Terry seems immature for this grade. Schoolwork is almost more than he can handle. Terry needs to study his times tables. Terry daydreams too much and doesn't follow directions."

When I was in fourth grade there was a popular sixth-grade teacher I never had. I'll call her Mrs. Y. One morning our teacher left the room to talk with Mrs. Y about something. While the teacher was away, the goofs goofed off. I pulled the chair out from under a friend. He fell on his rear end and started crying. The same friend had tried the prank on me minutes earlier, only I was quicker. I admit what I did was wrong, and I should have been punished. Our class tattletale toddled down to where our teacher was and told on me. I was summoned to the sixth-grade room, and this popular teacher kept me. My own teacher returned to our class.

Mrs. Y placed a paper grocery bag over my head and shoulders. The sack had a stupid-face painted on it she called "Pinhead." She stood me in front of her classroom for maybe twenty minutes while her giggling students went on with their lesson. I remember vividly what it felt like inside that paper bag. I was humiliated. When Mrs. Y's class went on break (it must have been before lunch or recess), she paraded me down the hallway still wearing the stupid-face sack, so other students could see. Mrs. Y led me back into my fourth-grade room so everybody there could have a good laugh. Then she took her sack and left.

I've always wondered if this teacher gained her popularity by sacrificing certain kids' self-esteem. I'm sure it wasn't an isolated incident, because she kept her sack. What she did would have destroyed some kids, but it just made me angry. One of my major character flaws is that I hold grudges far too long. After that fourth-grade experience I steered clear of her, and she ignored me. My short stint under Mrs. Y's thumb influenced me deeply. I gained a passion for the underdog, and an unflinching dislike for unbridled authority. Over the years my anger has mellowed and I've learned to redirect my emotions into a sort of fuel for my creativity. I've also developed a great respect for education. Teaching truly is a sacred profession.

Politicians who criticize public schools for not performing well don't know what they're talking about. They should follow me around for a year. Public schools are doing a great job amid the cultural values that produce the children they have to work with. Schools are one of the few institutions that are holding our society together. I've worked in the wealthiest districts and the poorest. In some districts schools are the only healthy community children have. Kindergarteners start off with the ABC's and end up as seniors reading Chaucer, Shakespeare and Whitman. That's a slow-motion miracle.

Flashback

In fifth grade I ran into my first good teacher, and the bottom fell out. It almost hurts to look at that report card. The grades are all D's and F's except for three C's in handwriting and three C's in spelling, which is puzzling. I'm not a good speller. I finished up the year with and F in Language of all things, and an F in arithmetic. I received a D in all other subjects and was held back.

I wrote about my fifth-grade experience in a poem called "Daydreamers" when I was a freshman in college. What a brash poem from my youth. I still wasn't following directions very well. I was supposed to be doing homework. I first self-published the poem in a chapbook. It became popular with professors in education during the 1970s. After I dropped out to study on my own, rumor got back to me from a student-friend that a professor had written the poem out on the blackboard for students to read. It speaks for a certain kind of child that still gets left behind.

A few years ago after performing poetry at a high school in Michigan, a sophomore girl named Leslie came up to me and said, "I want to tell you something about your 'Daydreamers' poem."

"What?" I asked.

"The teacher in that poem is my great-grandmother," she said, "and she wants to see you."

"I don't know where she lives," I answered.

"I'll draw you a map," was Leslie's reply. Later in the day she handed me a piece of paper with perfect directions to her great-grandma's house.

My fifth-grade teacher, Louise Corner, still lived just west of my hometown and north of the cemetery, but I didn't visit her. My personal take on our two years together was that we had a personality clash, as well as me being a poor student. The next year I was back at Leslie's high school. I didn't have anything to do one night, so I attended a girls' basketball game. At halftime while standing in the popcorn line, I ran into Leslie and her mother. We talked for a while, and Leslie's mom said, "Please visit my grandmother. She really wants to talk with you."

Well, I didn't. Anytime I was working in the Marion schools I forgot or ignored the request.

A few summers ago, as Mom was rapidly declining from Alzheimer's disease, my wife and I drove her to Marion to sightsee and visit my maternal grandparents' graves. As we left the Helmboldt family plot, I noticed a headstone close by. It was the grave of Louise Blevins Corner Furkey, my fifth-grade teacher. I'm wise enough now to understand the favor she did for me by holding me back. I was finally in with the kids I should have started kindergarten with, and school was much easier for me after that, though I was never a good grades machine. I patted Louise's headstone and said thank you.

Terry Wooten's second Grade class photograph from Marion Public Schools.
The poet is second from right in the top row.

The last time I visited my hometown I told this story to a group of sixth-graders. Their teacher Mrs. Fox raised her hand. She told me that her sister took care of Louise during the last year of her life, and that Mrs. Corner Furkey was very disappointed that I wouldn't visit her.

Mrs. Fox's comment made me feel pretty low. I realized I'd blown it. I wish I'd had gumption enough to visit my old fifth-grade teacher, and take along a tape recorder like I use in the Elders Projects. I wonder what our conversation would have been like. What insights she may have given me about myself. What a poem she might have been. What a lost opportunity. I'm sorry Mrs. Corner.

In sixth grade I experienced the first of my two favorite teachers. At the end of the year she wrote a short note to my parents, and placed it in my report card full of C's, except for straight B's in reading. It read: "Terry has proved quite a challenge to me this year, but I truly have enjoyed working with him. He is capable of doing much better work than he does, but at present he is much more concerned with having a good time than completing his work. He has a pleasant personality and is always good natured." It was signed, "Imogene McCrimmon." I was always good natured because I had immense respect for Mrs. McCrimmon, and sensed that she liked me, though she was tough. Up to that point I'd never felt that way about any other teacher. I'd always been more interested in having a good time.

Two secret worries I carried through these years were my ever-present fear of death, because of my epiphany about time, and a childhood depression that haunted me from growing up during the Cold War. In sixth-grade world history, when we studied the early chapters on Mesopotamia, Ancient Egypt, Greece and Rome, I had a hard time concentrating. It frightened me that those people had been dead for so long. I've gotten over that fear and depression as much as one can. It's where the humor in many of my poems comes from. One of my favorite Mark Twain quotations goes something like, "One of the greatest weapons humanity has is that we can throw back our heads and laugh."

In the spring of 2009 I was invited back to my alma mater to be the keynote speaker for the graduation ceremony. A few days before the event, Mrs. McCrimmon sent me a congratulations card telling me how proud she was. Reading the card aloud to my wife, I started crying. Teachers can really have a long lasting hold on you.

The big turning point for me came from reading one banned book, Henry David Thoreau's essay "Civil Disobedience" and another novel that students were warned about. A teacher, Sonja Titus, was hired at our school to teach high school language arts. All grade levels were still in the same three-story WPA building back then. Younger kids could observe what was going on at other levels, and be influenced, either in a positive or negative way.

Sonja was like no other teacher I had ever experienced. Turned out she was a closet beatnik. After she got the job, she frosted her hair. That was pretty radical in the early 1960s. Mrs. Titus also liked wearing tight, form-fitting sweaters that were cool at the time. This kept the non-literary-type boys interested in her classes. Her husband was a writer who had a goatee and worked at a local radio station. He visited our class once and read some of his work. In the short time Sonja taught at Marion High School, she ignited a creative renaissance that affected a lot of kids profoundly.

When I was in eighth grade a controversy swept through our high school. Mrs. Titus had assigned her classes to read a novel called *The Catcher in the Rye* by J.D. Salinger. Word got around that the book was full of swear words. Some parents or school board members got together, divided the book up and counted the swear words. The book was banned.

I got a copy of *The Catcher in the Rye* and read it. I didn't care much for the book, but it was thrilling to read something so controversial. I thought the main character had a bad attitude. I did learn a new swear word though. I still use it to this day as a simile about cold weather. One interesting fact about Salinger's character Holden Caulfield – he was the first guy to wear his hat backwards.

Later that year I noticed Mrs. Titus' students carrying around a book called *Walden*. I thought I'd better get a copy of *Walden* and read that before was banned, too. I read what I thought was the first chapter, "Civil Disobedience." Actually it was an essay used as a preface to the book. At first I was disappointed that there weren't any swear words, but I read on anyway. Thoreau wrote the essay after spending a night in jail for refusing to pay six years of delinquent poll taxes. He claimed it was his personal protest against slavery and our country's controversial war against Mexico. Someone paid his taxes, and he was released the next morning, but the experience had a profound effect on him. Like I stated earlier, the essay's message was, if your government or people in power are doing something wrong, then rebel, but always behave more civilly than those you're rebelling against.

Mahatma Gandhi had used this essay in his stand against British colonialism in India. I would learn this in high school soon. Martin Luther King was using the same philosophy against racism and segregation in the United States. I was deeply affected by Thoreau's essay, and it played a major part in my stand against the Vietnam War seven years later. I was just a kid and had never been in jail in my life, but I'd spent time in the principal's office. I'd also been paraded around the school hallway with a grocery bag over my head. I decided I wanted to be a writer like Henry David Thoreau. I wanted to disobey civilly. The book *Walden* was never banned, and my wish procrastinated for a few more years.

I think I was a freshman when Mrs. Titus assigned another novel, *Lord of the Flies* by William Golding. Our principal actually visited classes to talk about the book. Some parents and students were complaining that it was awfully depressing. The school board didn't officially ban the novel, but students were told they didn't have to read *Lord of the Flies* if they found it too disturbing. I read it, and later read two other books by Golding.

I loved the way Mrs. Titus spoke and enunciated her words. I wasn't in her inner circle of thoughtful and articulate students like the debate team and theater group, or the young writers who published a collection of poems, *What Is What A Million Isn't?* My cousin, Janice Helmboldt, had a poem included with the word "hell" in it, and compared the shape of a snowdrift to the curve of a woman's breast. That caused a mild sensation. I was an outsider looking in. I was the football player, but Sonja made me want to do better.

Mrs. Titus made us keep a journal with two entries a week. The writing had to be our own thoughts, or you received an incomplete.

After the first marking period full of incompletes, I tried harder. A door opened in my mind and it never closed.

Honoring Elders

Lifelines is Jack Miller's tale about experiencing the Bataan Death March, and being a prisoner of war for all of World War II. Jack was my mother-in-law's oldest brother. While growing up, my wife and her siblings were always told never to question Jack about his POW experiences. His own children were warned against this same curiosity. So for 57 years Jack kept his experiences to himself. With his grandkids, grandnephews and grandnieces things began to change.

Writing the poems for *Lifelines* in 2002 and 2003 changed the structure of my poetry, and that has carried over into what I call The Elders Project. *Lifelines* was the first time I'd written in lined poetry using somebody else's voice from tape-recorded interviews. With Max Ellison's story, *Words Wild With Bloom*, I composed from familiarity of his voice and from memory, much like I teach kids to do, except I wrote in prose.

In 1998 I received a Michigan Creative Artist Grant Award for writing a series of poems on the people and places of Michigan. The last rambling poem in the series germinated from a session I attended with my high school daughter and two friends to conduct an oral history interview with Jack. Out of curiosity I went along. During the interview it became obvious that the young ladies just didn't get it. Jack reminded me of the trickster rabbit in *Watership Down* who had journeyed underground to do battle with an evil one. When he returns with spiritual ears, nose, tail and whiskers ... having lost his physical ones in a battle of wits ... none of the younger rabbits remember him, or why he had left years ago to save them. This younger generation's amnesia about the war and what Jack had experienced bothered me.

I returned to interview Jack many times, once with my old friend Glenn Ruggles, who helped ease Jack into talking about some of the more painful memories. At my wife's urging, I added his wife's Leda's story about waiting for him at home, not knowing if Jack was alive or dead for the first two and a half years. The narrative was so gritty I had to create a new structure to make the poems accessible.

I used a poetics that I teach students, except with more stanza breaks, widely varying line lengths and less emphasis on what I call "power words" at the end of the lines. It makes the poems very readable or eye friendly. Seeing the poems in short segments encourages the reader to enter the narrative. The text is less intimidating and the reader can concentrate more on the story. A major difference between my earlier poems and the poems of *Lifelines*, *Child of War* and the Elders Poems, is that they're written using other people's actual words.

Child of War grew directly out of *Lifelines*. Since our country had invaded Iraq, I wanted to challenge myself and show how war affects the psyche of a child, in this case a little girl. I tell students I've never been a little girl before, or in a war, so I had to find a person who had that experience. I found her in the audience of a high school stage production of *Lifelines*.

Hannie (Prins) Kuieck is now a grandmother. She is also a close friend and a Stone Circle regular for more than twenty years. Hannie had never told me about her childhood in the Netherlands. During

Wooten performing at Lakeland Elementary, Elk Rapids, Michigan, 1985.

the first five and a half years of her life, she grew up under Nazi occupation. On the spot Hannie agreed to do a series of interviews out of which *Child of War* was composed using the same writing style as in *Lifelines*.

What I call the Elders Poems came from a new workshop I developed called The Elders Project. It evolved from what I'd learned writing *Lifelines* and *Child of War*. I wanted to get students involved with this interviewing and writing process. One of the tragedies of our modern society is that we've separated our elders from our youth. For thousands and thousands of years, kids listening to their elders, is where our histories and "herstories" came from.

In the Elders Projects, almost all the interviews are conducted by middle school and high school students, who are paired up with an elder from their community. After the interviews, the students are required to write a poem or two using the elder's own words. I then transcribe the rest of the tapes, and write poems around the students' work.

I've run into situations where the students tapped into a good story, but didn't ask enough questions. Maybe the elder got a little too emotional about a subject, and the kids shied away. In cases like this I often did follow-up interviews on my own. The Iwo Jima poems and "Peace" were composed in Stanley Holzhauer's words this way.

The Elders Project is a good blending of literature and history. In 2013 it won the State History Award in Education from the Historical Society of Michigan.

In the Elders Poems I try to stay as honest as possible to each individual's vernacular. It's interesting when you listen closely to people while transcribing taped interviews. Everybody uses language a little differently. This folk style of poetry can involve some grammatical problems, but unless they're extreme and would be embarrassing to the subject to see their poor grammar in print, I don't alter their voice too much. I do rearrange their words and energize pronouns and verbs though.

Writing poems from Elders Projects hosted by schools and communities around the state has propelled my art into another strong creative surge. I'm writing more now than I ever have. I get a lot of satisfaction from using what I've learned in forty some years of writing to help other people tell their stories. At this stage of my life I need something more important than myself to serve.

During the summer of 2013 a film crew from Barcelona, Spain, spent six weeks at Stone Circle shooting a documentary of my career, and to celebrate thirty years of poetry, storytelling and music at this unique forum. The big filming nights were August 10th and the 17th. It was a busy time hosting the crew and poet-friends returning from around the country to be interviewed and perform. One woman flew in from Rome, where she taught at the International Academy. She first recited poetry at Stone Circle when she was seventeen.

I was humbled and honored by this reunion. I did my first interview sitting on the boulder where I'd held our daughter, Blaise, to start the gathering thirty years before.

Terry Wooten
Elk Rapids, Michigan
November 2014

Part One

"There was a child went forth every day
And the first object he look'd upon he became,
And that object became part of him for the day,
or a certain part of the day,
Or for many years, or stretching cycles of years."

– Walt Whitman

Cubby the Fox

I own an old black and white photograph
of a red fox standing in high grass
beside my ten-year-old mother to be.
She's wearing a white dress,
kneeling and holding a thin leash
or long stem.
The fox is leaning and looking away.
I can see love in Mom's young girl body.

An uncle gave her the kit
after he found a den littered
with chicken and other domestic bones,
and killed the wild mother.
The pet fox had his own coop and freedom,
but liked to run inside the house.

Once he ran away with a fairy-fox-lady
for three days and nights.
Mom was heartbroken.
Riding around with her parents
in their car,
searching ghost towns, gravel pits
and two-track roads,
the family spotted a fox loitering
alone in a field.

I imagine him haggard and forlorn
like the knight waking
from the lady of the mead's spell
in John Keats' poem
"La Belle Dame Sans Merci."

They stopped the car, Mom slid out
and called his name.
The fox ran over and jumped
into the back seat beside her.

He rode back to their house
and lived as happily ever after
as a wild fox can.
He was Mom's first son.　　■

November 20, 1948

I was born in Mercy Hospital: Cadillac, Michigan
at 5:59 in the morning on November 20, 1948
　　starsuns in Scorpio. It was rain snowing
and stillwhite dark out.
It was deer season. Outside you could hear
but nobody listened. Cars were hissing
their rubber coils up and down wet icy roads
　　conveying hunters with their death loads
to hunt the graceful deer
sleek shy wild.
Hot guts and bowels sloshed inside stomachs
running back and forth in their forest cages
　　steaming to escape
away from this man animal
instincts could sense was on the prowl.
Ancestors howled in heart poundings
and tongues panted their brain sweat.

Guns started firing about the time I started dying.

Fear is the parent of insanity. And that night
I raced crazy through wilderness thoughts
of thousands of brains.
Last thing I remember is wondering where
the tree leaves blew to.

Somewhere outside, in the weeping snow falling
　　under a ghost tree

on the frame of a forest shadow
in the spirit of morning; a doe lay bleeding
warmth in the cold, dreams clotting to snow.

My head got stuck in my mother's birth pelvis:
her panting was crushing my skull.
The doctor had to uproot me from her womb
    by clamping a machine to my head.
By accident he tore my flesh.
With my first breath I began to weep.

I had one black eye and my mother almost died.
She couldn't see in this world for three days:
only feel my lips suck sweet milk of her swollen breasts,
my mushroom body pressed flesh
against her sweaty chest, weak arms fingering
delicate hand prayers over ribs
    touching her warm stomach for comfort.   ■

Totem

It was Spring,
a foggy day
full of different shades
of greens.
I hadn't realized yet
that I was alive.
Always been a slow thinker.
I remember
walking with Mom and her sister
across a field or meadow
gathering mushrooms
our way came to a turtle.
I didn't know
what it was.

Listened to the women,
felt the trill of the word.
The texture of its shell
looked like a rock.
Animal without a head
or any legs?
I peeked in a hole
and met two shiny eyes
scowling out at me.   ■

Me

When I was young,
sometimes I'd stand
in front of a mirror
and look at me.
Looking at me,
I'd think
I'm Terry
I'm Terry
I'm Terry
until I wasn't anymore.
I'd get afraid
and go outside
and play.   ■

1955

Mom kept saying
the real Davy Crockett had been homely.
She even showed me his picture
in our encyclopedia to prove it.
But the "Ballad of Davy Crockett"
kept right on going,
and was on the Top Ten for six months.
It was bigger than "Sincerely"
by the McGuire Sisters in 1954.
Then the movie came out.

I had a six-inch stack
of Davy Crockett bubblegum cards,
two Davy Crockett T-shirts
and a Davy Crockett lunch pail.
Mom wouldn't buy me a coonskin cap,
so I wore my faded red football helmet
with a fox tail tied on back.

Rock 'n' roll was busy being born
and I was six years old
riding along in the back seat
listening to Mom and her sister
talking over the music
about all those crazy girls
writing love notes addressed
to some young dead guy named James Dean
buried in Fairmount, Indiana.

Just then the gossip that would be legend
veered off in another direction.
We bounced across the bridge
over the Middle Branch River,
and almost levitated over my favorite hill
in the road on the other side.
I felt my stomach dance with my heart.

I stroked my Davy Crockett helmet,
and straightened my bubblegum cards.

Epilogue
James Dean died September 30, 1955,
entering eternity at precisely 5:45
in the afternoon at a crossroad
halfway between San Francisco and L.A.,
right where the San Andreas Fault
sheers through San Luis Obispo County.
The news spread like an earthquake
among the young across the continent.　■

Jesse James and Me

Dad worshipped the Old West.
I grew up on sermons about shootouts
at the OK Corral and the Little Big Horn.
We watched TV Westerns
with the same religious fervor
Great-Grandma watched Oral Roberts.
Even owned a Colt 41 pistol,
the same exact year, make and model
Billy the Kid had carried.

Dad's den was full of guns
dating back to colonial times
up through World War II,
but the Old West was the fulcrum
of the collection,
along with some arrowheads,
peace pipes and a bowie knife;
plus a framed picture out of *Argosy* magazine
a cheap Charlie Russell imitation
of cowboys, Indians and horses

lying around stiff and wounded
after an all-out brawl.

Jesse James was a famous cowboy outlaw.
He robbed trains and banks
and gave half the money away
to needy people,
and kept the other half
to help finance the myth.
I wanted to be just like him when I grew up,
at least my older cousin convinced me I did.

To begin our careers we broke
every window out of dad's barn
with my brand new Easter ball bat.
It was great fun, full of daring predictions
about our future fame and crime sprees,
until our imaginations cooled down.
Then we hid out in the hammock
out by the old walnut tree.

Later, Dad came in the driveway from work,
and let out a blood curdling,
"Who done it!" scream.
We split up!
My cousin took off east back home
to his old identity.
I headed north towards the woods.
Now, I could pace up and down the road,
back and forth across the fields
under the hot summer sun,
with a pebble in my mouth
to keep from getting thirsty,
just like Geronimo.
I had hideouts in every stump and stone pile
along the way,
but I was no match for Dad's anger.
He caught me halfway up
the first glacial moraine,
and licked me so hard I wet my pants

and got both cap guns too damp to fire.
Defenseless and whipped
I was herded back home
where I helplessly watched
the lynching of my new ball bat.

Dad threw it away out in the field so hard
that when it hit the top strand of barbed wire
Above the woven wire fence,
it spun around and hung there
tangled in a perfect noose
by the force of its velocity.
I was impressed
even through my tears.
It hung there almost a year,
with the wood weathering bone-grey,
and developing fossil like cracks.
Finally, under the influence
of another spring fever
and the Detroit Tigers' preseason,
I gathered nerve enough to ask for it back,
and Dad gave me another tryout.   ■

The Good Old Days

He was strong as a wild man,
though only a boy.
He left a trail of bloody noses,
torn coats and busted belts
all over the school playground …
until one winter recess
all the big guys united
in a snowball war against him.

To make the battle fair,
they gave this doomed warrior

all the rest of us boys
from fourth grade on down.
I was in the second grade and was drafted.

This modern day Attila the Hun
lined his army up
along the west sideline
of the practice football field.
He stood at the center
as our leader.

The fifth- and sixth-grade boys
lined up along the east,
facing us with flashing steel eyes.

I was on the far left flank
near the end zone
when we charged.
I saw the two armies crash into each other
like a bad accident.

I hadn't read yet, of Alexander the Great,
Hannibal or Tecumseh.
I hadn't discovered Steven Crane's
Red Badge of Courage.
The whole experience
was like a terrible *deja vu*
from a past life.

My second-grade courage deserted
through the goalposts,
and sneaked off
towards the swings and teeter-totters.

By the end of recess
I'd composed myself
and was standing near
a bruised, sixth-grade enemy hero.
He was crying

and holding his belt buckle
in three pieces.

By the next winter
this mysterious, scary sad boy had moved
on like a storm
to some other school playground.

Our snowball fights returned to normal
with an occasional bloody nose
trail leading to a school bathroom.

I was in the front wave of a charge
around the corner of the school building.
My mouth wide-open
around a barbaric vowel
must have looked like a bulls-eye.
An enemy sharpshooter
scored a perfect hit.

It was like swallowing a miniature glacier
traveling at the speed of light.
The snowball cut and gouged
all the way down to my stomach.
My third-grade buddies
carried me into the school
choking and gasping
for warm air.

That week the principal
and teachers banned snowball fights
forever on school property.

Young warriors died hard.
It took a week in the principal's office
sitting on the floor,
writing 1,000 times,
"I will not throw snowballs
on school property,"
before five of us signed the peace treaty.   ■

Nightmare

I walked across
the dew on the grass
behind the house
to Grandma's garden.
The morning fog was soft and silver.
The sunlight was young as me.
Little birds were yawning,
and the trees were vibrating
in a gentle wind.

Around the corner of the barn
a swarm of tiny yellow bulldozers
was plowing around like a plague
of machines ruining Grandma's
strawberries, string beans,
cucumbers and tomato plants.
I tried to stop them,
but there were too many.
They growled out of my hands and arms
like Stephen King toys
programmed to develop something.

Retreating through the wet grass
into Grandpa's barn,
I grabbed a gunnysack
and charged out the door
into the sunrise
back to the garden.
The rest is a nightmare
of catching little yellow bulldozers
and dropping them
into a snarling burlap bag
until I woke up.
Years later
I'm still wrestling this dream.   ■

Winding like Sirens

You could hear the train's scary whistles
winding like sirens through the woods,
warning the little city miles away …
the steel thunder gathering closer and closer,
rattling through old Indian burial grounds
lost in the woods
Grandpa told me about,
but I never found.

I'd drop whatever I was doing
and run down a gravel road
fast as I could past Peggy Jackson's.
The crazy woman;
she'd shoot at kids
with a BB gun
if they strayed in her corn.

By the time I reached the railroad
the whole ground was starting to shiver
from the diesel pulse serpenting through.

My heartbeats were scared birds
perched upon old skeleton buildings
so my eyes could see
level with the trains
as they came roaring round the hill
right at me
before swiveling past
on blurry caterpillar wheels
that could crush a penny flat.
Or me!

Once I stood on the tracks
and flirted with that idea,
then jumped free.
Standing there counting
the rollicking boxcars,
I saw a hobo ride by.   ■

Spike Horn's

There was a magic place
called Spike Horn's Bear Camp
located just south of Harrison
on old M-27.
It was the only place
in lower Michigan
where a person could feed or pet a black bear
without zoo bars between you and the animal.
Bears like poets
are some of the most unpredictable animals.
The police finally closed
old Spike Horn down
for safety reasons.

I was there only once in 1950 something.
It was the day after they carted
old Spike Horn off to jail
for a week
for hitting a cop over the head
with a frying pan.
I can't remember seeing any bears.
They must have carted them off too.

I bought some postcards and a pennant
that are collectors' items.
They show old Spike Horn with a Rip Van
Winkle white beard,
and flowing white hair.
He's feeding full grown bears
from his hands and mouth.
He's sitting on a stump with two little girls,
letting the littlest feed
a huge black bear from her little hand.
He's standing with his favorite bear
posing hand in paw
in the middle of thirteen uneasy people.

He's gone,
gobbled up by the red tape of a new age.
Old Spike Horn has passed on
in the parade of time,
and so have his bears.
And now the tourists can breathe
a little easier.   ■

A Shining Suit of Armor 1412-1431

In the fourth grade,
sick at home missing school and watching TV,
I saw Joan of Arc appear
out of the Middle Ages
across the afternoon movie.

A hundred years of war.
The map of France was bleeding
from English victories.
Northeast of the wounded land
in the backwoods along the Moselle River,
a teenage girl kept hearing voices
while walking in the woods
past a fairy stone under a sacred tree.

Something told her she was the answer
to an old prophesy about a young woman,
a Maid from the Lorraine Mountains
who would save France.
Joan wasn't too pleased at first.
She cried and pleaded for an easier job.
Her voices said, "Go!"

Ms. Arc cut her hair short,
started wearing men's clothes,
and rode off to end 80 years of losing.

The peasants flocked behind
their young goddess incarnate.
She told the lazy prince,
"Make the most of me,
I'll last only a year."

Riding a white horse and wearing a shining
suit of armor like a warrior witch
Joan of Arc changed the momentum in battle
after battle against the spooked English,
until she was captured.

They locked her up in a men's prison.
English churchmen and a few toady politicians
found Joan of Arc guilty
of being too spiritually creative,
dressing like a man,
sassing her elders
and consorting with fairies.
Heresy, sorcery and witchcraft.

Joan told her judges that saving her soul
was her own business,
that wearing men's clothes
while living with men was common sense,
and wouldn't deny her fairy friends.
She also begged for a women's prison.

They gave her a choice,
to burn at the stake
or live in a men's dungeon wearing dresses.
Joan talked it over with her voices,
chose a man's habit and fire.
I didn't understand the church bells ringing
as her smoke rolled into the clouds,
so next day I looked Joan of Arc up
in a school encyclopedia.

The English left
and the war ended.

The big Church granted a retrial
and found Joan's legend innocent.
In 1920 Joan of Arc was declared a saint,
489 years too late,
but it's the next best thing
to living happily ever after.   ■

Behind Main Street

Marion Public Schools had a library,
but it didn't compare with
visiting the dead pioneer lady's house.

Busting out of the backdoor of the school,
escaping for an hour,
we'd race down Water Street
over the nameless creek bridge.
Taking the shortcut through the ghost spaces
of old Clark's and Chadwick's Mills,
past the Mill Pond and swimming hole,
pausing to pay respects to
the timeless brown water
now the Middle Branch River.
Scrambling up the embankment
we'd cross M-66,
and sneak through the lumberyard warehouse.
Like wild deer
we sensed a trail
older than the roads and buildings.
Jumping the railroad tracks
we'd scurry up the hill path
back into the grid of Western Civilization.
Crossing Chadwick
we'd follow Fourth Street east
to Pickard, turn right
and walk to number 217.

After calming ourselves,
we'd enter politely
through the jingling door
into the late Mrs. Alice Chapin's home
now a memorial library.
A dining room, kitchen,
utility and living room full
of shelves full of books.
The good smell of books,
the feel and sound of books
when you opened the hardbound cloth covers
into the crisp pages.
It felt like church
only more relaxed.   ■

Elegy for the Carl D. Bradley

Six hundred and forty feet
of riveted steel judged unsinkable,
the big freighter Carl D. Bradley
steered northeast away from the shelter
of Wisconsin's shore,
working through hurricane force winds,
twisting and thumping in a wild arc
across northern Lake Michigan
headed home to Rogers City
after the last haul of the year.
Ugly green 30-feet high waves
thundered against the starboard hull.
November 18, 1958,
the grey light disappeared
into howling black snow clouds.

The 30-year-old long boat
could carry enough crushed stone
to fill three freight trains

a hundred cars long,
but she'd rubbed bottom
near Cedarville two weeks before.
The cargo holds were full of rust
and she'd been popping rivets all day
from the strain of the storm,
but this was normal.
The 35-man crew rode on below
out of the screaming winds.
At 5:30 the big ship radioed Rogers City
telling the wives not to worry,
that the waves were rough but routine.

Minutes later Carl D. Bradley
was lifted out of the lake
by a dark mountain of water
full of unbelievable power.
The old inland seas freighter groaned,
bowed in the middle, rocked up and down,
radioed for help, buckled
and broke into eternity.
Electric cables snapped and hissed,
men screamed and prayed
for their wives and kids and friends.
The hot boiler exploded in a death shudder
as the cold lake swallowed the ship's heart,
and through the icy night hours
all but two of the men.

Cars full of families from Rogers City,
Posen, Onaway, St. Ignace and Cheboygan
drove to Charlevoix.
They shined their headlights
like prayers out into the storm.
But the morning rolled in
full of fatherless children.

Fourteen years later a faded life ring
from the Carl D. Bradley washed ashore
on Pelee Island in western Lake Erie.   ■

Daydreamers

I failed fifth grade. My teacher said
I daydreamed too much,
That I didn't pay attention to her
arithmetic, science, English, or history when
I should have.

Had her all over again
in the same room
with the same windows
to dream out through
the next year.

She said the very same
things all over again,
but I passed anyways.
New friends was all.

She's still saying the same
things I didn't care to listen to,
and failing daydreamers
inside the same room
with those same windows
I dreamed through
   to way out past her windows
waiting for failures' dreams to come true.

The Blessing

The varsity basketball star glowed
in his sweaty practice jersey.
He was all-state, gifted but different,
the closest thing to a Greek god
in our little town.
Number 24 lounged back

in the locker room folding chair
like it was his throne.
Three sixth-grade boys swarmed around
invading his space.

Success hadn't spoiled the athlete's moments.
He leaned forward into them,
adjusted his shoelaces,
reached into his duffel bag,
took out a piece of Dentyne,
wrapped in a stick of Doublemint
and pushed the gum whorl
with his sensitive forefinger
between his smiling teeth.

Two sixth-grade wannabes begged for a piece.
The third boy held back.
He couldn't dribble or shoot,
but often stood in front
of the closed ticket booth
admiring the maroon and white
plywood tote board conference standings.
The woodblock town names and numbers
of wins and losses hung like legends
from metal hooks.

The third boy had his own imaginary
basketball league and radio sports station.
He played all the games in his head
and broadcast the scores into the night
as he fell asleep.

Wide awake now
he gathered his sixth-grade courage
and asked the basketball star
for some gum too.
Number 24 handed him
his last piece of Doublemint.
The shy boy rolled the gum on his tongue
savoring the taste of the moment.   ■

A Rose Red Dress 1926-1962

A Marilyn Monroe calendar
hung on the wall in Dad's den
below his antlers and pistol collection.
She wore a rose red dress,
and if you lifted the plastic overlay
it erased her clothes.
Presto! She was lying on her side
her entire profile exposed.
My friends and I used to congregate
in front of Marilyn's sideways smile
daring each other
until we wore the overlay out.
We had to glue it back on.
After that, her dress hung a little crooked.
You could see the rim of Marilyn's skin
shining out around the edge
like a sexy eclipse.
It made the calendar even better,
until Mom cut out some women's undies
from the catalogue,
and dressed Marilyn up like a paper doll
underneath the overlay.
Marilyn Monroe's calendar introduced me
to the abstracts of romance
and the thrill of being.
After the calendar year ended
Marilyn hung around without any months,
days or numbers under her toes
like a rim walking flesh goddess of eternity.
Dad moved her to his workshop
out in the garage.
The plastic overlay fell off again
and got lost or tossed away.
The paper doll look disappeared.
Marilyn returned to her 1949 perfection,
but I missed the rose red dress.   ■

The Hank Williams Bug

Hank Williams in his prime
once stopped his limo
on a bridge over a river traveling
somewhere through rural America,
and dropped a hundred dollar bill
in a little boy's hand
just to buy his fishing pole
so he could sit down
and dangle his tired old cowboy boots
over the bridge
and fish a while.

Dad had the Hank Williams Bug.
He liked to fish, drink and sing
country-and-western songs,
and host fish fry parties
so Mom would play her piano
and Dad his guitar
while their grown-up friends
hovered and danced around
acting funny.
Mom played the guitar too.
One night Dad got loose
and roughed up one of Hank's songs
with his voice
sounding like his hot rod
roaring out of the pits.
I don't remember the words,
but I was impressed.

Mom had been an aspiring musician
before she met Dad.
She was gifted.
She could play any song by ear,
and liked to sing so much
as a little girl she would sneak
into the back pews at funerals
to participate in the hymns.

Except for their parties
and trying to play rock 'n' roll
for us kids,
getting married pretty much finished
Mom's musical ambitions.
As for Dad, the drinking
and Hank William's songs
gradually overtook him,
but without the limos
and the hundred dollar bills.   ∎

A Different Kind of Dark

When the fighting got real loud
my sisters and I would shiver out of bed,
turn the lights on
and cry and stare at each other
in front of the cracked mirror.
It was a different kind of dark.
When Dad started hitting Mom
we'd gather in the light bulb glare
and scream out of harmony
down the stairs
for him to quit.

But Dad had alcohol and steel in his head,
and Mom, our own personal goddess,
wasn't wise enough
to figure out how to stop it.

So it went on for years
mixed in with the good
revolving around Mom and Dad
cuddling on the couch,
while we danced around
like love manifest.

The joy and the hurt were so sharp
and constantly cutting against each other
that they dulled both edges.
Us kids survived the pain
like an autumn game
of dodging falling leaves
on a windy day.

I've got a winter photograph
of an old sunset sinking
behind our white, two-story farm house.
In my mind I know every space
of that old home
that doesn't exist anymore.
Mom and Dad were divorced
longer than they were married.
Dad's motto always was,
"I ain't no twelve-stepper."　　■

Snowball

One black man, a good-natured hermit
lived northwest of town
along the railroad tracks.
Everybody called him Snowball,
except the elders.
They called him Tommy Banks.
Snowball didn't have any birthday,
birth name or family.

A circus found him
way down south
in what was left of the Confederacy.
He was a sad, little, lost bundle
crying beside the road.
The circus people were in a hurry.

They didn't have time to help him,
and they didn't want to leave him there.
So they took him.

Old man McGinn, who managed the circus,
vacationed every summer southwest of town,
and eventually died there.
That's how Snowball ended up here.
He made a living
cutting firewood by hand
for 50 cents a cord.

This was before Malcolm X went down
like a crucifix sprawled across *Life Magazine*.
This was before Martin Luther King
climbed to a peak of consciousness
with his gentle, powerful march of words.
This was quite simply before
we had to have an excuse
for not knowing any better.

My dad gave Snowball his birthday
so he could get a summer job
on the Michigan Gas Storage pipeline,
and the guys down at the corner gas station
baptized Snowball around a fire hydrant.
That was after they filed a petition
to get him out of the county jail
over some entanglement
with a white woman.
The guys were more protective after that.

By the time I was a kid
Snowball was an old man with a beard like Moses
and eyes of a clown.
On summer holidays he would dance
on broken glass,
swallow knife blades
and eat fire sticks.
He was full of old circus tricks

just like April Fools' Day,
which became his official date of birth.

Snowball died
in a home full of senile white folks.
And he grew senile
right along with them.   ∎

Noon Whistle

The old religious woman
said she voted for him
because she figured he'd start a nuclear war,
the Second Coming in her mind's eye.

She was tired of living
and wanted to meet her maker,
only she didn't want to do it alone.

Her God's morals were medieval
and old fashioned,
but he dressed modern.
I saw him once in a nightmare.

He wore a welder's helmet
like an executioner's hood.
He held a melting torch in one hand,
and a hissing arc in the other.
His fire was so bright
you could see your bones.
Soldiers lined up
to witness him
groaned.

The noon whistle
always sounded like an air raid,

and served to remind me
of the dangerous times
I'd been born in.

Nuclear War was the super bogeyman
that kept me awake nights.

My childhood depression festered.
It got so bad I took comfort
in that the whole population
would at least die with me,
including my TV heroes.

To keep my fears company at night
I listened to my AM transistor
pocket radio.
I could plug the whole country
from New Orleans to Boston
into the side of my head.
Lying there in the blankets
in a dark house under the stars
I first discovered Mr. Tambourine Man
playing a song for me
at 3 o'clock a.m.   ■

The Slipknot Affair

This First Class Boy Scout
going for Eagle,
needed a new challenge.

I'd take a rope to bed
and practice my Boy Scout knots.
Tying myself up was a regular tryst
while waiting for sleep.

I was good at
binding my hands together
or my feet to my hands,
and wriggling loose within minutes.

I could hear Mom and Dad downstairs
watching TV and getting ready for bed.

Tied a slipknot
around my right wrist,
and a two half hitch
loop for the bedpost.
Lashed my left wrist
to the left bedpost
with a simple clove hitch.
Slipped my pre-tied right wrist
over the right bedpost,
and there I was
snug as a bowline.

I worked at getting loose
halfway through the 11 o'clock news.
The right slipknot was cutting
off circulation.
A clumsy left hand
couldn't slip free
of a simple clove hitch.
My feet were flopping
out of frustration.

Just before Johnny Carson
I gave up
and called for Mom.
I still flinch from the bright truth
of my bedroom light
being turned on.
Mom called Dad,
our Troop 56 Scoutmaster
upstairs to see too.   ∎

A Perfect Moment at the Mill Pond

She was fifteen, shaped like a woman
in her swimsuit
to me at thirteen.
In front of all the other guys and Mom,
this downstate girl
agreed to meet next afternoon
at the swimming hole in town.

I arrived three hours early at 9 a.m.
She noticed me cruising my bike past
her family's vacation cottage.
As I walked down the path
she came flirting up around the bushes.
The dew-damp green,
heart-shaped leaves
were sighing.

I panicked and turned back up the hill
to fiddle with my handlebars
and gather composure.
She followed smiling
and joined me beside my bike.

A beautiful fifteen-year-old girl
with a river voice
and peach-colored skin
was caressing my handlebars.
The blood splashed through me
like water down the fish ladder.
Fifty years later I remember everything
except her name
and the color of her swimsuit.

We stood on the earth dam by the Mill Pond
in the chrome sunshine
like a Beach Boys' song,

only this was mid-Michigan
and she was from Pontiac.

Soaked up the day and each other
swimming and lying on a blanket.
We skipped lunch.
Mom ruined it at 3 p.m.
She picked me up to work in the hayfields
for money I spent.
I still save this girl's voice
and how the sun and water glittered on her.　■

First Kiss at the Sun Theater

We'd been going steady for two weeks
and still hadn't kissed.
I wasn't bored
with her or the movie,
I was just yawning.

Stretched my eighth-grade arms
like lovebird wings,
my left arm settled back down
gently around her shoulders.
She quivered
but didn't pull away.

An hour later my arm was numb
and the movie was almost over.

A pounding heart urged me on.
"Do you mind if I do something?"
I whispered tenderly.
"What!" she asked.
"Kiss you." I sighed,
and made my move.

I couldn't move in like a goldfish
with my eyes wide-open.
Closed my eyelids
and leaned towards her.

Clink! My front teeth hit something.
A small piece of tooth broke off,
slid over my lip
and tumbled like stunted popcorn
to the dark floor.

My eyes jarred agape
saw her glass Coke bottle
raised between us.
"It wouldn't be right," she said.
Wounded, I didn't argue.

The rest of the movie was a blur.
After The End
I walked her out of the theater
to her dad's car,
and watched her chauffeured away.
I felt like my piece of tooth
on the littered floor.　　■

I Wonder What Life Would Be Rated?

Elaine and I liked each other
in the eighth grade,
but never admitted it
face to face or in love notes.
Her single mom
(who worked at the Horseshoe Bar)
and my dad
(who drank too much)
were having an affair.

Ours was a doomed infatuation
and we knew it.
We were more mature than our parents.
Young passion was just as real,
but not as greedy.
We remained flirting friends
and let the air ache around us.
I wonder what life would be rated?

One sad, grey, autumn afternoon
Mom trailed Dad's red pickup
through town to Elaine's home,
a dark-haired woman with him.
As we skidded into the driveway
to block Dad's exit,
Elaine jumped out of his truck.
A ride home
as favor to her mom.

Hurrying across the lawn
to her house,
Elaine glanced over at me
slouched in Mom's passenger seat.
She looked down
and ran inside.
Our romance never had a chance.

It was almost a relief
when Elaine's family moved south,
but awful lonesome in class
sulking behind Elaine's empty desk,
wondering where
my wife was
in the future. ■

Dysfunctional Love Poem

It was that do wa diddy time
of summer and life,
when the days buzzed
and the nights were full
of giggling love and misty moonlight.
Blood rock 'n' rolled through them,
but she didn't love him anymore,
least her mother wouldn't let her.
So he left the dance,
walked downtown alone
and banged his head
against the hardware store.

He shrugged it off.
He took to wearing leather,
and grew his hair like a grumpy porcupine,
sort of an expression
of his spiritual state
and a bumpy home life.

James Dean had been dead for years,
but it didn't matter.
Teenage girls who had once
written love letters to James in his grave,
were now mothers
of teenagers full of rumblings.
There were lots of other girls
in the county.

He and his favorites
would climb the old abandoned fire tower
at night
to survey the territory.

Some kind of weird magic was happening,
especially on Saturdays
when the dance club opened.

Only problem was
you had to keep your shirt tucked in.
The stars at night
revolved like a hit record,
but she didn't love him anymore.

He was getting used to the feeling,
and liked the freedom.   ■

The Prime Sisters

I dated two sisters from Grand Rapids,
and had a crush on their mom.
It was a bonanza family for me.
I met the big sister first
posing on the beach
at Rose Lake
in her candy-striped swimsuit
pretending not to notice
us Boy Scouts.

On Old Fashion Day after the parade
we made out beside the Mill Pond
and her wrinkled blouse.
We kissed so long we got bad breath.
I didn't know
you could get bored doing this.
She was the wiliest.
She wouldn't go steady
or help push my motor scooter
up the hill to Sunrise Lake.
She had a city boyfriend
with a fast car.
So I switched to the younger sister.
We fell in love for a week,
but lived too far apart

except in summertime
when the Prime women moved north.
The local girls hated
how they attracted attention.

I could talk to their mom.
When I drove the furniture truck
into the furniture city
to pick up a love seat or hide-a-bed
in the spring
the sisters were in school.
I'd stop by their house to visit anyway.
One hot May morning
I surprised Mrs. Prime
ironing clothes
in the kitchen
in her brassiere.
She put her blouse on
and fixed me coffee as usual.
She was my first girlfriends' mom
who treated me with trust and respect
when she knew I didn't deserve it.   ∎

Mr. Prime Laughed With His Wife Till 3 A.M.

We weren't Peeping Toms,
just teenage guys sprinkled with moonlight,
tiptoeing up the wooded driveway
of the Prime sisters' summer cottage
to make sure those Grand Rapids boyfriends
weren't there.
After Mr. Prime heard us
it was easier to run
than try to explain.

Our driver and other friend riding shotgun
spooked and peeled out
leaving us stranded
between his taillights
and Mr. Prime's headlights
coming down the driveway!

Mr. Prime wouldn't quit
trying to catch us.
We sneaked along the road
and hid in the ditches for two hours,
watching our driver's midnight '50 Ford
hotrod back and forth every half hour
trying to rescue us,
but always in the dusty headlights
of Mr. Prime's station wagon
in hot pursuit.

At 11 p.m. the Ford retreated
back to town with a broken motor mount,
the water pump fan sawing into the radiator.
We didn't know this until the next morning.

At midnight Mr. Prime
chased us off the road again
into a little moonlit valley woods.
My partner lost his shoe
in a black hole full of mud,
running through an invisible creek.
He had to dig it out by hand,
and swore at me for laughing.
Then he surrendered
to Mr. Prime's spotlight,
and gave him my name.

Mr. Prime knew me
and started calling
my direction in the dark,
so I surrendered too.

We rode home subdued in his station wagon.
To ease my embarrassment
Mr. Prime complimented the midnight '50 Ford
driver's driving.
I almost got grounded,
but was right back out with his daughters
that weekend.   ■

The Platters Dance Club

Eight years earlier
they tried to ban anyone under 21
from dancing to this kind of music.
A New York newspaper read:
"25 Vibrating Teenagers Hospitalized
After Dancing To Rock 'n' Roll All Night!"

Nothing like that ever happened to us
at the Platters in Cadillac, Michigan;
but when you walked through the doors
something powerful in the music started
working on your brainwaves and heartbeat.

For three dollars admission
for three hours a week
you could become the dream
of who you were or wanted to be.
All around the huge wooden dance floor,
that had been a roller rink
before rock 'n' roll,
there was a loose hub of dancing,
breathing, sweating, pulsing teenagers
surrounded by more young people
cruising to 45 RPMs
like a brand new wheel of life
rotating almost out of control.

A physical renaissance was in the air,
and your parents were home watching TV.

In the summer you could dance outside
on tile circles set in cement
surrounded by trees and a wooden-rail fence
with soft yellow, red and green lights
blinking up into the night
like romantic traffic lights.
I didn't meet my wife there,
but I tried for four years.   ■

Motorcycle Parable #1

Buck Lacord wasn't interested in grades,
or inspired by report cards.
He was the best athlete in school,
the highest high jumper
and fastest dasher,
but he was never eligible.
So he raced his dad's car
up and down the country roads,
until he bought his own motorcycle.

Buck used to stay overnight
when he was younger.
In bed he'd lecture in whispers
on the necessities of a successful life.
I'd listen,
though I hardly ever agreed.

Around ninth grade
Buck started a local chapter
of the Hell's Angels motorcycle gang.
He was the only member
and it only lasted for a day,

because his spelling wasn't too good.
Buck rode proud
all over town that day
with "Heel's Angles" emblazoned
in big bold letters
across his back.

Lesson: It takes a little education
to be almost anything in this world.   ■

Motorcycle Parable #2

Coach smoked Newports,
so I'd smoke Newports too.
I liked the mint-colored
spiffy boomerang shape
on the package,
and that sensual magazine ad
of the pretty woman
in her sexy-summer dress
pulled up above her knees
wading in the sparkling creek.

My parents were gone for the day.
I dug up my cigarette pack
wrapped in a plastic bag
hidden under the water tank.
I fired up my Cushman motor scooter.
In my imagination
it was a Harley Davidson
robin's-egg blue.
I stripped off my T-shirt,
lit up and rode off into the immortal wind,
posing over my handlebars
for the river goddess.

Without a windshield
the cigarette burned like a fuse
spraying tobacco sparks
all over my angel face
and hairless chest.
A painful quarter mile
down the rebel road
I pulled over
and put my cigarette sparkler out.

Lesson: Do not smoke cigarettes
while riding a motorcycle
without a windshield.   ■

C Minus

Right in the middle of his geography report
on South America,
while we were all busy taking notes,
Jerry Bowens, the wiry left guard
on our football team
stopped …

After a nervous pause
we all looked up in his direction
towards Venezuela and Colombia
with our ink pens ready
for the next fact,
just in time to see Jerry pass out
in front of the map
and collapse to the right
off the portable podium
towards Ecuador.
He rolled down the teacher's desk
through Peru,

his left hand grabbing at Bolivia
and crumbled out of sight
in the direction of Chile
ripping a big earthquake and landslide
through the map as he went.
We heard his head bounce
against Argentina,
then a low primal moan
oozed out from under the desk
from Uruguay and Paraguay.

While the teacher and one alert student
helped Jerry Bowens out of the room,
three little countries,
Guyana, Surinam and French Guiana
hung on by a few threads
from the roller above the blackboard.
We all just sat there staring
at what was left of Brazil,
hoping that this would at least delay
the test on Friday.   ∎

Undefeated

The ambulance was always parked
along the sideline
as our football team unloaded
thundering off the bus
like a stampede of Sir Lancelots.
It didn't scare us.
We were young and tough,
immortal as a dream,
except for our ex-wide receiver
who'd died in a car wreck between seasons.
This senior year was for him.
The school band rattled and boomed
and the cheerleaders bounced
around pumped up athletes
making clumsy declarations
for victory in his honor.

Last year's undefeated season
had ended with a win in a rainstorm
and a wrestling celebration in the mud
that had been the 30-yard line,
then more horsing around
outside the locker room.
Before coach made us quit,
I was wrestling our wide receiver,
my friend,
trying to stuff cold wet leaves
up his jersey and down his pants,
making him into a soggy scarecrow,
feeling his laughing warm against my face.
It was the last time we ever touched.
New Year's Eve he was dead,
crushed under a seventeen-year-old car
that for an instant must have felt
like a huge football helmet
illegally spearing him in the back,

while our lives rushed on
like an 88-yard touchdown run.

The ambulance was there that night too.
Before the police made me leave,
I watched our broken friend
lying motionless on the frozen gravel road
under the flashing lights
and immortal old stars.

We went undefeated again
and dedicated the trophy
to his memory or spirit or something,
but he gave me a more personal gift
to remember him by;
a small scar on my right elbow
from that rainy-autumn night he tackled me
on the wet leaf-stained cement
outside the locker room
to celebrate.   ■

Good Question

Never really thought about why
I keep a stuffed horned owl,
a harbinger of death to some people,
perched on top of the maple hutch
overlooking the rooms of our house.
When I was young enough to get away
I stole him from my dad
who'd brought him home to use
as a decoy to hunt crows.
I eloped with the beautiful bird
to my room upstairs,
and Dad never followed.

Old Dusty Feathers has been with me
ever since.

Death and I grew up together.
He wore my Boy Scout hat,
neckerchief and merit badge sash
when I wasn't using them.
He tried on my graduation cap
and went away to college with me.
He wore my poetry bandanna
and wooden beads.
Now he wears my Stone Circle amulet.

A mythic decoy of death
perched on top of the maple hutch
I inherited from my dead grandmother,
staring over the kitchen table
I inherited from her too,
doesn't spoil my appetite.
He keeps me on my toes.
He makes me wonder
what it was like to be an owl
alive and wide awake
hooing under the foggy stars
into sleepy ears
a long time ago.   ■

Terry and Wendi Wooten following their wedding,
Torch Lake, Michigan, September 20, 1975.

The Wooten family near Stone Circle, 2014.

Part Two

"But the beauty is not the madness."

– Ezra Pound

Got In an Argument Over Harmony

After playing cards with a deck of Tarot
   the young witch
gave me a magic-wooden toad
to keep me company
                  on the journey.
     This silent night
   all I know about astrology
is an instinct
feeling out
towards so much sparkling space,
          so this is the path I take.
Is there such a thing
     as a mistake,
or are there just choices?
   My life has become a fork in the road.

Any straight line
               becomes a circle
if you follow it far enough.
Just ask Einstein.
Walking along the highway
watching the car lights go by like meteors,
I've grown
to know loneliness is a quiet well
           that forges a self
like a teaching fire.
          Confucius says:
"While you are not able to serve men,
     how can you serve spirits
of the dead?
While you do not know life,
how can you know about death?"

Never saw the comet
          except in a dream.

Pacing 4th Avenue
            out of frustration
I hear a baby crying
      how I feel
about not being able to say these desires.
            It reminds me
of the first people
to draw language into an alphabet,
how they copied patterns of stars
for the shapes of their letters.

Got in an argument
            over harmony
with a beautiful disciple
from St. Louis, Missouri,
   who supports her enlightenment by modeling
at an art studio downtown.
            Never seen her nude,
            but I'd like to.
Still, I see no reason
to be satisfied with the world
as it is,
just so we can look peaceful and radiant.
We sipped tea
            that makes your body hum
         over the rhythms of life
and talked about sun seeds
till around midnight.
            Then she grew awful quiet
so we could listen to each other's thought waves,
      but I got nervous
      as an earthquake
and ruined the whole affair.   ■

Wild Horses

A herd of wild horses are stampeding through my head.
Their hooves hammer clay to dust
pounding for sunset horizons.
Tall blades of golden grass wave out of their way.
Long manes flag,
hairs whip the air,
and nostrils flare in my brain
insane for freedom.

Eyes storm out of dilated visions.
Reasons are a cloud of sand.
Sweat foams from their muscles
beneath raw leather coats
   racing to a pile of bone rattlings
adrift on a desert ocean.

It seems you have chosen tame horses
over these crazy colts that trample through me;
that you would rather ride the ones with a mildness
in their wild streak,
But that's okay.
Wild horses were getting restless for new pastures anyway.

Someday
after mountain teeth have bit their last breath
and lie choking at sunset
with jawbones full of sand.
Someday
after tongues have turned to clay,
bones weathered to chalk stones,
and you have your own tame horse ranch.
Someday
after freedom's ghost has run off into tomorrow …

my only wish is
that you will turn three chestnut mares and one stallion loose
for freedom's spirit to call them home.   ■

An Hour

I'd been working in a ditch with the sun
all day at $5 an hour
                    pouring cement
for the base of a storm basin.
   Around 3 p.m.
a dragonfly started buzzing around my head.

Something about the sound of his wings
woke me to his body
so green it seemed blue.
As he landed
in front of my attention,
I reached out with a welcome finger
and the dragonfly climbed on.

Brought him up close
to see what was the matter,
                    and discovered
two splashes of cement drying on his eyes.
He was rubbing them with his feelers
asking for help.

I apologized by laying down my trowel.
Taking out my handkerchief,
I wet the corner with spit
and spent the last hour
helping him clear his vision;
while the bulldozers plowed around us,
and the cement trucks revolved.   ■

Jeffrey

My Cape Cod poet friend
combed his hair the way he woke up,
and liked to wear
catsup and mustard stains
carefully splashed
on the front of his shirts.
He never wore shoes
except in cold weather,
and hung a wrinkled tie like a noose
around his neck.
He was in mourning
for his dead younger brother.
For a long time
I kept a painting of his
created by filling small glass jars
with pigments,
and throwing them against
a cement wall,
letting the colors bleed down
over the canvas.
He was a better poet than I,
though he never wrote a poem
while I knew him,
just obscene chants
to stay in shape.
His only ambition
was to write ten great poems.
Like most friends, in time
we just drifted apart.
He died in a car wreck
driving home after a party
to celebrate *The Paris Review*
publishing his first.   ■

A Vision

It's noon
and I have a vision
of the ghosts of Sitting Bull and Tecumseh
sitting in pow wow
with the spirit of Walt Whitman and Jesus
    Christ passing the peace pipe
in a cloud over Washington, D.C.
Outside the phantom tepee
an atmosphere of Henry David Thoreau waits
in solemn grace,
while the skeleton of Geronimo spits his teeth
at the sun.
On the edge of this cloud
Crazy Horse fasts,
    meditating on horizons.   ■

Six Miles North of Key West

This morning I woke up horny with life;
    so wandered down by the sea
to squander my time
for the shore's
heart of water. I swam in the wet pulse.
The waves stung my eyes like sweat or soap does.
Crying pleased
I crawled out
on the palms of my feet,
and stroked the sand with my soul. I kneeled
in the wind.
        Two seagulls blew over
wrestling with their wings
in a tug of war for a limp fish
dripping breath.

I watched them
and thought about the politician's inauguration speech.

Only wished to listen to the ocean's heartbeat,
but deaf war jets kept roaring over my world eyes.

To comfort my patriotic sadness I started reading
Walt Whitman's vision for our nation.
His verse howls.
The salty breath of his songs
inspires me! But damn it!
Walt quit scrawling our diary 80 some years ago.
(Many mortal truths have born out of his bones.)
          This ocean reminds me of the old poet's grave;
how waves sparkle under afternoon sun rays,
and seaweed "leaves of grass" keep washing in
on this flesh colored beach
laced with rotting driftwood trees
all polluted with tourist garbage.
          Sat surrounded by their crap most of the day
waiting for some wise voice to speak through my fingers,
    until I got bored.
So chanted what my guts had to say;
and walked home
with sunset on my shoulders.   ■

702 Locust Street

Glimpsed a falling starlight kind of ship
speeding through tonight;
as my ego was perched up on my roof
wandering
with the planets and suns
revolving across the universe.

Watched it glow away into a deep blue vision.
Then climbed to the peak of the house
to lie down
among moss growing between tile shingles.

On this shore of earth
traveling stars
are pulsing awful bright vibrations,
and my summer lady is two blocks down Locust Street
studying
her prehistoric to modern
Michigan archaeology textbook.
My constellation breezed through
her early to late pages
when the great lakes were waterfalls
and forests shallower,
before ages of ice swelled out of the north.

Many waves later
a spirit ambled when a copper skin people walked
paths now buried under years of leaves.

Bluebones, my hound dog son,
scowls out the attic window at my silhouette
and sniffs and howls,
"What's so interesting?!"
A bellow before the wheeze in his voice
his throat warbles
sounds like ancient poetry.   ∎

Wooten at Stone Circle, c. 1988

Part Three

"A lover gambles everything,
The self, the circle around
the zero! He or she cuts and
throws it all away.

This is beyond
any religion."

– Rumi

Blue

Bought an old faded green
                    pickup truck
and painted it light blue,
almost the same color as my hound dog's name.
Had 88,753 miles on it
before I ever put it in gear.
Those are all good numbers
because that was a lot of bumps in the road ago.
It's got a transistor AM radio
and tappets that rattle a bit.
    Bluebones likes to stare through the music
out the window
for rabbits or squirrels along the way,
while we ride back and forth from work
to support my profession of poetry.   ■

Erich Rehwinkel

When breath was young as the wind
in his eyes,
            before the world wars began
a young man
immigrated across the worried water
to America.
The brothers he left
in the old country
were shot by the government for evading the draft.

Now the old German's eyes sparkle,
    but his teeth don't;
and though he forgets things,
    he knows.

Erich is a carpenter by trade,
one of those highborn kind
with hands that shake from years of patience,
and a mind that works
like a great level of thought.
While time speeds up
and the world tilts in its gravity,
his energy moves real slow
     to balance
the space in between.
Death leans on him like a tired friend,
and he likes to spend his age
arguing with a new breed of lumber yard clerks
who all look the same
to him
over the low quality of boards
and high prices.

Been helping him
          build a roof
and cut down some dying elm trees
at his homestead across Green Lake
from Interlochen Arts Academy.
          We've become pretty close comrades
with the hammer and saw.   ■

The Swan

All fall
     the road to work traveled by a small lake
just after the curve
     before Wicks Lumber Company.
There one swan breathed
alone.
He appeared one cold bright morning
like the dew,

about the same time the leaves began to rain.

Driving by every morning and evening
I grew quite close to him.
He reminded me of my guardian angel
                              and love,
the way he swam proud lonely circles
between the shores
    with his great wings relaxed at his side.
At night
I can imagine how
the stars sparkled over and below him
              in the water
       at his center of his universe
framed by bare trees in their winter drowse.
He calmly paddled
watching the light turn to snow
              falling,
and ice begin to thread across his wake.

Venus burns over the horizon
about a hands reach above the sunrise.
In late November
              as I drove by,
my friend was walking on the ice
that had formed during the night.
By sunset
              he'd left,
flying off like a myth
into somewhere deep and warmer inside me.   ∎

To Wendi

Swans were flying all over the place
this spring thaw.
The mute-white birds,
their hearts beating like deep drums
mate for life;
or if one dies
the other spends the span of its wings alone.
So the afternoon before I met her
when a few flew over my eyes.
Well.
Swans don't have to buy a marriage license
or have blood tests taken from their pulse.
They don't have to buy a house
or pay rent either.
They just sail and sleep together
in the waters
under the stars.
That's why they make such good omens.   ∎

For the Edmund Fitzgerald and Crew

The front great wave of winter
blows over the night.
       Stars brace themselves.

It wakes my dream
out of bed
at the open window.
The trees
bend
way down.

Morning is still blowing.
I've got the day off so take a walk.
Rolling clouds head
southeast all day.
Some birds spread their wings
   on the high air.

Twenty-five foot waves last night
on Lake Superior.

In Chicago
windows blew out of the tallest building
in the world.   ■

McLachlan Orchards

Plowing for the farm,
    the clouds agree.

Plastic ear mufflers
protect my inner ear hairs.
I can hear myself
feel
the tractor's working roars
        lugging tugging
forged steel blades
vibrating through the ancient earth.

Wham   now and then
into a billion-year-old stone.

Pick them up
into a pile of time,
all the things that rocks have gone through.

       My back bones ache.

Tiny sparrows and one great lake gull
flirt along
    in front of the tractor
hunting
for grubs to eat
in a hurry.

Blowing rain shadows and sunny shy birds
drift over.

Will plant corn and fruit trees.   ■

Zen Hunting Poems

Bought a bow license
        in a taxidermy shop.
Hundreds of dead birds and animals
were mounted
in dull fur and feathers
on dusty shelves.
Their stiff shapes
stared out of glass eyes
at me
and three other guys
in matching camouflaged hats.

Haven't hunted for eight years
so get a bow
to start out with.
Guns are too loud.
Hunting the deer's ways
as much as the meat
I sit so quiet
porcupine stumbles over my feet.

The woods have a rhythm
the deer belong to.
They walk like good dancers.
It's hard to hear them sometimes
when it gets quiet inside me
my heart beats
affect the rush
of sound through my ears.
Every pulse
is like a deer stepping.

A yearling with long skinny antlers
appears.
His graceful grey body
walks over my sight.
I'm not hiding very hard

sitting on a fallen elm.
He notices
something alive about my shape.
Breathing
staring at each other
his dark eyes look for what I am.
Mine keep blinking
He picks his way closer
sniffs some air
looks me right in the eyes
then turns and walks away
careful
not to hurry
disappearing in the trees.
I wonder what I smell like.

Rub a ripe apple all over me
and try to blend in
with some scrub apple bushes.
Watching the valley
full of wild apple trees.
Pick out a favorite
sixty paces
down the hill.
When apples fall
my heart thumps.
From here you can see Torch Lake.
The sky's reflection
changes different blues
with the weather.
When it gets dark
comfortable lights come on
across the water
and stars come out.
I sit in the cold and watch.

In a blizzard
I visit Lake Michigan's shore,
wild and white ice statues
of wind and water shapes.

Should know better
but raise my arms wide open
towards the northwest
and let out a challenge singing yell.
The storms spirit swells
and bellows back
powerful as a locomotive.
I cower
behind some cedar trees
and apologize.

The next day
while hunting,
the wind keeps teasing me
drawing deer shapes
with branches and weeds
to trick me
in the corners of my eyes.

Clouds full of snow
storm over
all week.
I buy some warmer gloves.
The deer paw for apples
and walk quietly
with white backs.

5:30 in the morning
is too dark and early
to hunt deer
except with my ears.
Lying back on the cold ground,
the old stars' suns
aren't a very warm blanket.
The moon is shaped like a smile.
Its reflection is
in my coffee cup.

Just before sunrise
the first day
of rifle season
is dark as a deer's eyes.
The stars begin disappearing
one by one
like the deer.   ■

Crow Dance

On the road
out front of our house
a male crow does his spring strut dance
for the lady crow of his choice.
Daylight glistens brand new
full of soft, damp colors.
The crow's shiny, black head bobs
up and down
to the mating rhythm
inside him.
He steps
real fancy,
a kind of march.
Lady crow pecks at the gravel
beside the road
watching him
out of the corner of her eye.   ■

Full Moon

The phone jangles me out of sleep.
Like a weird dream
I fumble my way through the night
to the noise.
It's my pen pal,
an old friend,
a sister or wife from a past life
calling from Maui via satellite.

Her voice wakes me up
from 12,000 miles away.
She wants to know what time
it is here.
It's two in the morning.

I've been lazy about writing.
Our lives have been drifting apart.
She's still lonely,
looking for that permanent man
in this life.

We talk for an hour and a half
about her problems,
my poetry
and pottery glazes of ancient China.

After we hang up,
she walks outside
and sits on her front porch
to watch the moon come up.

I go back to bed
to get some sleep,
but the moonlight is shining
through the crack in the curtains
on my face.　　■

Grandma Heim

Grandma Heim's Midwestern roots
were three generations deep.
She didn't want to die
way out in California,
except all her kids were out there.
So she was stuck
living the last three months uprooted.

If it hadn't been for the protests
of her exotic granddaughter
who flew in from Maui,
they would've hooked her up
to a life support machine
and prolonged the agony.

No way did she want to be buried anywhere.
Cremation was the only answer,
except she made them promise
not to spread her ashes
around among strangers.

The children didn't want to send
Grandma's remains home alone.
They felt she belonged with family.
So she was a problem in a jar
on a shelf in the hallway.

There were two solutions.
Grandma always loved roses.
They could pot her under a rosebush.
Or better yet,
they could make her into a work of art,
a piece of pottery.
But none of the ancient, oriental glazes
her granddaughter was experimenting with.

So now Grandma Heim is a stubborn,
little antique-type jug
with Midwestern lines
the color of plowed earth
in the morning sun.
She sits on a shelf
in a little Polynesian house
in Paia, Maui,
looking a bit out of place
surrounded by too much oriental art.
But she's always within reach
of her favorite granddaughter.   ■

Heartburn

Walked outside the restaurant
after eating a shrimp special,
all I could eat.
My belly felt fat as the full moon
hanging on the horizon.
Three drunk Indians hitchhiking
out front where the road forks,
split up arguing.
I stood on the front steps and watched
the oldest with barbershop hair
stumble off by himself
trying to thumb a ride.
The other two,
wild young men
with crow black hair
long as high grass,
started pushing and shoving each other,
both falling into the ditch.
Smiling white people's heads
kept gliding by
inside nervous windows
rolled up.   ■

Short Poem and Ten Tankas for Ezra

seed of mine
tucked in my wife's egg
like a cocoon
growing like a pollywog
through the whole of evolution
in microcosm
getting bigger and bigger
like a miniature whale
rubbing against Wendi's insides
bumping her kidneys
I lay my hand on her belly
and it seems to come
to the warm
where my hand is
and rub against the feeling

the night lights shine
on my sleeping wife
uncovered
the child I planted is still
small as a star

those midwives are all right
but so young
there's a whole generation missing
progress terminated
like so many other living things

life passing through time
from uterus to uterus
generation on top of generation
like tree rings
or top soil

been thinking about my ancestors
a lot lately
wondering way back

same atoms that composed them
now circle in me

while driving
I catch myself humming
like grandpa used to
an old song
I don't even know

something powerful in a flock of geese
passes over
subtle as a pulse
frogs start singing again
the stars look like their voices

rain pounds the road
clouds thunder
but under the pine tree
in front of our house
the storm is sifted to a mist

fish slippery as love
full of sperm and eggs
swim up the rivers and creeks
the moon is crescent
shaped like a pregnant woman's belly

the magic
in life
is hard
to see
like a morel mushroom

carrying my first born
into the herbal bath
everybody says look
at the sunrise
but my son is brighter   ■

For Bluebones

Hugging my hound
at midnight
in our driveway
made of gravel
stones wet with dew,
wondering what Blue thinks about
life beyond
bones and wishes,
food and itches,
my hugs and kisses
under the northern lights.

Epilogue
Goodbye grumpy old bachelor hound
with a car and raccoon crucifix scar,
and crooked front legs
from the motorcycle
that ran over your puppy bones.
Goodbye old one-eye.
I suppose you chased
a deer right past Saint Peter
into the happy hunting grounds.   ■

Willie

By the end
Willie was nothing but
a knotty skeleton
lashed together
by stubborn old muscles
wrapped in worn out, burlap skin.
He was one of the last
of the old wolverines,

and he'd worked right up
to the final harvest
in his son-in-law's garden.

Willie had worked hard all his life
and wasn't afraid to say so.
When he said so
he'd get right up in your face,
and the words would fly
like a thrashing machine.
But he always had good breath
so it wasn't so bad.

Willie never had much money.
He just liked to plant things
and watch them grow.
In his heyday he never knew
much about birth control.
His family resembled a miniature city.
Out of necessity Willie became
pretty good at cutting corners.

This was back when
doctors still made house calls.

The doctor came again one night
to help out with another birth.
To give Willie something to do
he handed him his medical instruments
and told him to sterilize them
in some hot water.

A half hour later
the doctor couldn't
find his instruments anywhere,
and Willie was out in the barn.

The doctor had been
on the road all day
and was hungry,

so he helped himself
to some bean soup
simmering on the stove.
That's when he found his tools.

Willie had the only
daughter in the county
born with the aid
of medical instruments
sterilized in homemade bean soup.　　■

For Blaise

My writing is being overrun
by family life.
I've got tiny bulldozers
on my bookshelves,
toy tractors in my desk drawers,
and Wendi's belly
is tumbling again.
Her pelvic bones cradle
another life.

It's a girl!
Born on the tail end
of a sunny spring day
she comes out purple,
but pinks up soon enough
taking little sucks
of bright oxygen,
peeking out at us
with one eye.

Ablaisia! Ablaisia!
She's my girl!
She's no bigger
than a fox squirrel!　　■

Summer 1983

Took Ezra down to Lake Michigan
full of shiny stones.
We threw some flat ones on shore
back into the water.
Full of wishes
we ran laughing
through the clapping waves.
Ezra danced
a three-year-old's dance
of ecstasy
on the lips of life,
while I watched.

This is the summer
of 90-degree winds
that blow hard as blizzards
turning leaves
upside down on their stems.
Our ten-week old daughter
studies them
puzzled.
Fifty- and sixty-year-old men
start to act old.
The white caps roll in.
The field corn shrivels.   ■

Part Four

"Forty years Bob's been away,
But his trees are wild with bloom today."

– Max Ellison

Words Wild With Bloom
An Oral History Poem Biography of Max Ellison

The title of these poems is by
my close poet-friend, Taelen Thomas,
from an adaptation of the last
two lines of a Max Ellison poem,
Old Bob's Been Dead For 40 Years.

The poems are for Taelen, who
edited and assisted me with this work,
and introduced me to Max in 1980.

Some of the grammar in these
poems isn't exact, but it's the
way Max spoke. In certain cases
I chose to keep the cadence of
his voice, as I remembered it,
rather than give in to some
grammatical rule. I think Max
would have liked that.

It's like the answer Max shot
back at a person who corrected
his pronunciation of the word
"herb."

"You mean 'erb' don't you?"

"No," Max said, "I mean 'Herb'!"

If you look close at the second star
from the cup, on the handle of the Big
Dipper, you'll see a faint star speck
about the width of a finger above.

That's the Test Star. The Ancient
Egyptians used it to test their eyes.
From where we are it looks real close
to the Big Dipper, but it could be
we're closer.

I slept in the park last night. After
the softball games I had a flat tire.
Then they turned off all the lights. So
rather than hassle with it, I just rested
in the car out under the stars. The police
came by about 2:30 to see if anything was
wrong, then went on.

Most of the lumber camps were gone
by the time I was born, March 21, 1914.
But they named me after a lumberjack
who still worked just off M-88 on The
Wildcat Road. I think he had something
to do with getting the doctor for my
parents.
    He was so proud the night of my birth
He started drinking to celebrate. Then
early the next morning, while hung over,
he tried to break up a log jam.
    But he made a mistake of wrapping a
logging chain around his body instead of
carrying it in his hands. Then he made
another mistake. He slipped off the log
raft.
    It took them twenty minutes to unwrap
the chain, and by then it was too late.
Especially from the bottom of the lake
on March 22. So we didn't share the same
name very long.

I remember every day of my
childhood. Every one of them.
We were poor as church mice.
I was born in a log cabin, just
like Abe Lincoln, in the same
bedroom my father was born in.
My first memories are of World
War I ending, a big picnic and
riding with my father in a
horse buggy, watching the sand
in the road get sucked up by
the wheels, then drop again. I
grew up amid the ghosts of
lumberjacks and surrounded by
pine stumps.

I was a shy boy with a phobia
about speaking to people. My dad
tried to cure me of the problem
by giving me messages to deliver.
I was fine until people answered
their doors. Then I'd panic and
run away. I started memorizing
poetry to compensate. I made a
vow to overcome my fear.
    First time I recited a poem
for an audience I was nineteen.
It was for a local entertainment
show in Bellaire. The poem was
"Gunga Din" by Kipling. I was so
scared and so dazed that I could
hardly find my seat afterwards.
Right then I swore that I'd never
do anything foolish like that again.
I kept that promise for thirty years.
    At forty-nine I was invited to recite
my poems to an audience in
Northville. It was common knowledge

that I wrote poems and memorized
them. I was also their garbage collector.

I was so nervous my spit thickened.
I could hardly speak, let alone say
poems. All through the reciting I was
praying for a drink. I never noticed
a friend set a glass of water on the
podium right in front of me.

Giles was his name. His house
is still standing across from the
old Bellaire golf course.

Giles would loan you $400 at
the drop of a hat, but try to buy
a dozen eggs from him and he'd
haggle about price for an hour.
If he didn't get what he wanted,
he'd store them upstairs.
When he died his upstairs was
full of eggs.

His barn was kept immaculate,
but his house was filthy. They
always joked if you could buy
your milk or cream from him
before he got it to the house,
you were okay, but once he got
it to the house, it was dirty in
an instant.

Everybody dropped their spare
cats off at Giles'. He had skinny,
half-starved cats all over the
place. Once I saw a kitten fall
into a full milk can in Giles'
kitchen. He just fished it out,
stripped the milk out of its fur
back into the can, and went on
about his business.

I was fourteen and feeling good from some homemade wine I'd been sipping. I wasn't really that drunk, but enough so that I couldn't go home. I was the janitor for the local dentist, so I decided to sleep it off in his office. Stumbling up the stairs I met the doctor coming down. His office was right across the hall from the dentist's.

"What's wrong Max?" he asked.

I couldn't tell him I was drunk for fear of my parents. So I said, "I'm sick," and started groaning. I settled on my appendix quick. Every time he touched that area I'd moan.

Damn if he didn't call my mom and tell her I was having a severe appendicitis attack and that he was taking me to the hospital to operate in the morning. I decided the best thing was to go along with him until I sobered up, then back out, saying it didn't hurt anymore.

But then the nurse woke me up just past midnight preparing me for surgery. Before I knew it I was in the operating room with the ether mask over my face. It was terrible.

So that's how I had my appendix out. But it was still better than if my mom had found out I'd been drinking.

In 1931 Bellaire was getting a little confining for me and a friend by the name of Glen Perkins. Neither of us had ever been out of the state of Michigan. But we each had a suitcase, and we spent half that summer packing and planning.

We decided to go to Florida, mostly on the merits of this huge rattlesnake skin that hung on the wall of the local gas station. The owner claimed it was from Florida.

A few days after Labor Day we took off hitchhiking and lugging our heavy suitcases beside us. Five days later in Cincinnati we were almost broke and a lot smarter. We got a job caddying at a golf course and slept in a dingy little room off a restaurant. After a week we took off again.

I remember hitchhiking out past Lexington on Highway 68, a fellow pointed out where they were having horse racing. That intrigued me. I made a silent promise to return there another year.

A day or so later, tired of hitchhiking, our heavy suitcases, and the hot weather, we decided to hop our first freight train in Pine Knot, Kentucky. We waited till after dark, then climbed on and went to sleep.

When we woke up we were rattling south. I hurried over to the open door and sat down. I was probably the happiest hobo in America. I only wished the train was going through Bellaire, so everybody could see me.

That was the beginning of my romance with trains, coal smoke and all. But from then on I traveled alone and without a suitcase.

By the way, we never made it to Florida. A bunch of hobos warned us against it. They said we'd end up on a chain gang. So we switched to trains headed back north and rode all the way to Cadillac. But the next summer I was right back on trains again.

It's like old Rome used to say,
"Just give me a horse that will
come in second place every time."
My love of horses goes way back

to the bones of Nell scattered around
the old farm.

When I was nineteen I got a job
feeding and grooming the race horses
that Fourth of July at the fairgrounds
in Bellaire. After that I was hooked.

I read up on horses the way most
guys do baseball players. Then I wrote
a letter to every well-known horse
trainer in Kentucky. Only one wrote back.
He said they didn't need any help, but
anyone who could write about horses the
way I could should have a job around
horses. So I headed on down.

I made a dollar a day, plus board.
For the next few years I lived, ate and
slept with horses. I even rode trains
with 'em. From racetrack to racetrack,
from New York to California.

Some people say I missed my true calling,
which was horses, but that's not exactly
true. I realized quite early that horse
racing was a rich man's game. They gobbled
up the best, and gave poorer men the cast-
offs. I never did like playing second fiddle.

I worked for an egg factory
out in California for a while.
I drove the boss crazy, because
I could remember a row of hens'
numbers, and which ones laid the
eggs, without having to stop and
write each one down separately,
which was company policy.

Then I practiced writing my
name backwards and let him catch
me doing it, while peeking over
my shoulder. That really drove
him up a wall.

What do you mean art? Oh yeah.
Sometimes I forget what I'm doing
is art. But there's money in this
here poetry. But then I'm the kind
of guy that, if I make fifty dollars,
I think I've got the bull by the tail.

So you've been to Japan studying
poetry and Zen monasteries. I almost
went to Japan once too, but they
surrendered.

Just before getting unloaded in the
Philippines, with the Michigan Seventh
Cavalry Division (like beef at the
slaughterhouse), to retake the islands,
I received a telegram from home informing
me about the birth of my first child, a
daughter. The war took two years out of
my life before I saw her.
Don't get me started. I'm full of
nightmare stories about going out on
patrol time after time with twenty-four
other guys, and being one of the few to
return ... about diving between two dead
bodies to escape machine gun fire ...
and getting feverishly sick, having the
hospital bombed three times, finally
recovering on my own while being carted
from shelter to shelter.
You can't imagine getting used to
smelling like a corpse and somehow
managing to stay alive. But enough ...
let's get back to poetry.
I like Whitman ... I read all of
Leaves of Grass in one week while

hunched in a fox hole. A Jap sniper
had already picked off two men before
me, so I kept my head low and read. And
when I did have to move, moved fast.

You sure see some funny wounds
in combat. I remember this one guy
lying there with a bullet hole
right through his helmet, and blood
pouring out. We left him for dead,
and went on gathering the wounded,
until he cried out.
    On closer look, the bullet had
ripped through the helmet front,
ricocheted off the strap clamp or
something, and buzzed around the
curve of his helmet, peeling off
flesh in a ring around his head.

I remember this one officer.
He gave me royal hell for making
friends with one of the natives.
He made me stand at attention the
whole time, and wouldn't let me
say a thing in my own defense. I
never got over my dislike for him.
    Six months later, one night
after our outfit had been ambushed
and shot up, I got to go with the
wounded back to the hospital. It
had been just an old vacant building.
    It was raining and the hospital
was pretty full. So I slept in the
hallway next to some dead soldiers
wrapped in plastic bags. There was
a faint light from the operating

room, and I noticed the dog tags on
one of the bags. It was that of the
officer who'd chewed me out.

The thing I'm most proud of ... there was
this hill on an island in the South Pacific
during the war. Not a big hill, but we'd been
trying to take it for weeks. Finally it was
me and eight other guys' turn to rush it. At
the top we ran into a solid wall of machine-
gun fire, so we turned and charged back down.
A couple of the guys were wounded.

Safe in our trenches we turned around and
peeked back up the hill. Damn! What we saw
was one of our men sprawled out right on top.
Well, we couldn't leave him there.

I never was the hero type. I was scared
all the time in combat with people shooting
at me, but for some reason I volunteered. I
took off fast as I could back up the hill,
landed face down in the burning dust behind
a little bush, next to the still body.

"Are you okay?" I asked.

"I'm playing dead," he answered.

He'd been hit, but not bad. He was more
disoriented about which way to get up and run,
so he just lay there too scared to do anything.
I decided to use his arms and legs like points
on a compass. First I asked him if he knew
where his rifle was. When he said no, I told
him it was three feet out from his right foot.
Our troops, I explained, were in the direction
of his middle toe on his left foot.

"Now," I said, "at the count of three grab
your rifle and run!"

In combat training they taught us to run
zig-zag like lightning, but if we had we'd be
dead. We ran straight back down the hill with

the bullets singing around us. Then they took
him off to the hospital unit.

Next day I was wounded and carted off too.
I ran into him while they were unloading me
out of the ambulance wagon. He grabbed my hand
and shook it and told everybody I was the guy
who saved his life. Then they carted me inside.
I never saw him again.

By the time I was twenty I knew
exactly what I wanted to do. That
was work with horses, hobo, steal
kisses and fish for trout. I liked
to write too. I was always writing
letters, long train letters everybody
said sounded like poetry.

Five years later, here I am in
the middle of a trout stream in
California, with America gearing up
for war all around me, and I don't
know anything except about horses
and writing. And there's this girl
back in Michigan.

So I hopped a train home and got
a job in a factory outside of Detroit.
From then on I knew exactly what I
wanted to do. That was go back to
Bellaire and buy the old Frog Holler
school grounds, and live down in the
woods and write poetry.

But I was locked into the war and
a woman and raising a family. It took
me thirty years to make Frog Holler
come true.

I know what it's like.
I used to collect garbage
seven days a week to feed
my pigs. Then sometimes I'd
buy 'em for twenty cents a
pound in the spring, feed
'em all year, then have to
sell 'em for eight or twelve
cents a pound, while trying
to raise a family.
   "Old Whiskers and His Hogs,"
they called me. That's a far
cry from what they write today.
But I thought up some of my best
poems during that period. I'd
just climb in my garbage truck
and throw my cares away.

   I used to write at the kitchen table
in the middle of five kids and my wife.
The ones who weren't screaming or fighting
on the floor with their noisy toys, had
the TV blasting. Finally we moved into
our own house, a bigger one, with room
enough for my own study. But after a few
attempts at writing in such idyllic quiet
and solitude, I gave it up and moved back
to the kitchen table.

   I'd heard the same woman
introduce Anne Sexton a couple
of years before as, "an author of
love poems and beautiful poems
for children." I said to myself,
"Lady, if you ever introduce me
that bad, you've had it."

Now here she was introducing
me to an auditorium full of high
school kids as, "a farmer poet
who writes poems about farm animals
and agriculture." I said to myself,
"Lady, you just blew it."
    I thanked her and started out
with this poem:

>   Jenny Miller bought a donkey
>   At a farmer's country sale.
>   She fed him all that winter,
>   Brushed his mane and combed his tail.
>
>   Spring, and all the fellers
>   From forty miles around
>   Know that Jenny Miller
>   Has got the best damn ass in town.
>
>   But she had to pass a rule,
>   And thereby hangs my tale.
>   All her friends can ride for nothing,
>   But her ass is not for sale.

    That got the kids' interest in a
hurry.

    They told me he died with my
book of poems on the nightstand
next to his bed. Too weak probably
to read it, or throw it away.

    When they told me my poems
weren't good enough for *The Third
Coast* anthology of Michigan poets,
I was so damn mad I drove all the

way home, composing an angry letter
on the way.

By the time I got back to Frog
Holler and copied it down, I wasn't
mad enough to send it anymore. But
I've got the letter. It's in the
Pauline notebooks. Some of my best
writings are letters in those
notebooks.

These academic poets, they make
the money and get the grants, but I'm
living the poet's life. I've sold more
books than all of them put together. I'm
the one out there with my sleeves rolled
up, doing the real work.

There are less than a dozen
poets in the United States who,
without any backing from grants,
universities, or whatever, have
managed to make a living off poetry.
I happen to be one of them.

Best portrait ever painted of me
was scraped back off the canvas
after the artist caught me with his
girlfriend in a very intimate way.
But they've got a good one in a gift
shop at Clam River Bridge. It's when
I was younger. The artist is dead now,
but he caught my hat and the way I
wear it tilted to the side perfect.
That'd make a good one for your cover.

Do you know what this red candle
is symbolic of? It's the source of
wax I seal Katie's letters with.
The symbol of my love.
    But I started to get a little
carried away and began sealing the
pages together and dripping it up
and down the edges. Finally, she
asked me to cut it out. She said it
was too hard to open the letters and
read them, while driving her taco
truck. Now I just use a red marker
pen instead.

    I got to thinking I wanted
to be a well-known poet, and
the best way to do that was
to get in with the kids. So
I started reciting poetry in
schools. Pretty soon one school
led to another. I've always said
if you want to get along in an
area, get along with the kids.
As they grow the rest will come.

    I walked into a bookstore
in Petoskey the other day, the
store one of my daughters manages.
They've got Jim Harrison books a
half-foot thick in a long line on
display. Do you really think he's
sold more poetry books than me? I
never met him, but I sold a book
to one of his daughters once.

I keep telling myself I'm not
going to jump up and down anymore
when I get to the part in *The
Star-Bellied Sneetches* where the
star-off machine jumps and bumps,
but then I do anyway. I can't help
myself. That poem has done me more
damage, physically, than any poem I've
ever performed. It's where all my
physical troubles started. I got
carried away and jumped off a step
in front of a stage. Right then I felt
something like a little spring snap
inside me, and I've been winding down
ever since.

I've got lots of hitchhiker stories.
I'm always picking up hitchhikers. It
gives me somebody to talk to. I picked
up this one guy and somehow the words
got around to women, but not the way
it's supposed to. This guy hated women.
As the miles rolled by he worked
himself into a frenzy over them. I'd
already extended an invitation to share
a motel room for the night, so I was
stuck with him, still ranting and raving
as we climbed into our separate beds.
Finally he settled down, or at least
was quiet. But every time I peeked over
at him, his eyes were glowing, red specks
in the dark.
Needless to say, I didn't get much
sleep that night. I made a vow to stay
awake until he went to sleep. But his
eyes never shut. They just kept glowing
red in the dark.

Finally around 2 a.m. I got up to go
to the bathroom and take a closer look.
He was sound asleep. What I'd been seeing
was his digital alarm clock on the stand
next to his bed.

I picked this one guy up in Virginia
and right away I sensed something was
strange about him, though harmless enough.
He said he was headed to Ohio to visit his
family, but I doubt it. Said he hadn't seen
them in years. I knew he didn't have any
money, so I bought him lunch.

Every place we'd pass, he'd bring up
George Washington and wonder if George had
been there, or what George had done there.
He was obsessed with George Washington.
This went on all day, until he finally got
on my nerves.

I let him out in Pennsylvania. I offered
him some money, but he wouldn't take it, so
I used a little psychology.

I said, "Now, George Washington always
paid his troops, didn't he?" He nodded yes.

"Well," I said. "I wasn't going to tell you,
but I'm George Washington." You should have
seen him. His eyes almost popped out of his
head.

"Now, you've been with me all day and I'm
going to pay you for it. Okay?" He shook his
head yes, in awe.

"Now, muster up!" I said, and he snapped
to attention. I went to the back of my
pickup (I drove a pickup back then), where
I kept a box of change, and counted out twenty
dollars worth. Then I took it up and handed
it to him.

"Now," I said, "about face!" He whirled

around. "March! Left, right, left, right."
And off he marched.

That's the last time I ever saw him, marching
down the side of the highway, with a big smile
on his face.

Between the motel room and the car
is a lonely space. And you're going
to have car troubles in this business.
You might as well get used to the idea.

I don't know much about cars either.
I drove my orange Volkswagen for a year
before a friend showed me how to use the
rear defroster. If a car won't start
it's either the battery, or it's out of
gas, but I can't tell the difference.

That's another thing about this Amish
hat I wear. It makes it easier for me to
get help when I need it. I just get out
and stand by the car looking puzzled,
and somebody always stops.

Once in southern Ohio, I lost my drive
shaft, or universal, or something. The
only lucky thing about it was a repair shop
half a block away. A couple of friendly
strangers helped me push it there.

The head mechanic said they could fix
it, but not until the next afternoon.

I said, "Fine, I'll wait." Then I went
outside and sat down practically on his
front steps, by the car.

After about an hour the guy came back
and said, "Maybe you didn't understand me.
I said we could fix it, but not until
tomorrow afternoon."

"No, I understand," I said. "I'll just
wait." He looked at me kind of funny and
went back inside.

About twenty minutes later he sent two
of his mechanics outside for the car. Three
hours later I was on my way. I probably
paid a little extra for it, but I was still
on schedule.

This elderly waitress full of
bad cheer ran a good restaurant
with an ill-mannered sort of tenure.
She refused to serve me coffee until
she'd brought the eggs I'd ordered.
This happened twice or more, so I
took it as a type of challenge.
Next time I passed through town,
I went there again. When she asked
if I wanted the same, I said, "Not
today, just coffee."
When she brought me my coffee,
I said, "I've changed my mind. I'll
have breakfast after all." You should
have seen her face.

My girlfriend is just a
skeleton laying in the ground,
but in 1928 she was my teacher.
I was so in love with her I
finally just let my feelings go,
threw caution to the wind
and wrote her a letter. I told
her exactly how I felt. She wrote
back, "You will be a writer."
We wrote back and forth every
day for more than a year. A couple
times she even kept me after school,
until my parents almost found out.
I was fourteen and she was twenty-two.
I figured it out from her obituary.

I've had my security pulled out
from under me so many time it doesn't
matter anymore ... Besides, they can't
pull it very many more times, before I
fall right over in the grave.

I suppose someday I'll be at some
high school reciting a poem and start
forgetting the lines, and the teachers
will think, "Poor Max, I can remember
when he could do that poem."

What these kids don't realize
when they see me dressed this way,
is that I'll be dressed the same
way tomorrow. I own one pair of
pants that I call my dress pants.
They are in bad shape. I have a
worse pair that I wear when I wash
the good ones.

Florence said to me, "Max, I
don't know how you survived these
last ten years ... two pairs of pants
and a half dozen shirts lying in
the back of the car."

I kept my old worn-out wallet
taped together with furnace tape
unraveling. That way it stuck
inside my pocket better and made
it harder for pickpockets.

His eyes have got
little dollar signs
tattooed on their lids,
and every time he blinks
it's like a cash register
ringing. He wouldn't even

consider driving his car
down a gravel road to get
to a poetry reciting.

    I have a style of my own
far off from the police beat,
down in the woods filled with
moonlight, snow and frost. In
a little house filled with good
smells, I write. The snow is so
deep and soft that even with
snowshoes I sink to my knees.
Today I worked on shoveling
my roof. Tonight I sit in my chair
and rock and cook and enjoy my
own company. Tomorrow I'll
make a path to my spring.

    I've got a sales tax number, but
I never use it. The Internal Revenue
Service was always sending me letters
inquiring why. I just told them that
I couldn't sell anything.
    Finally I wrote them a two-page
letter, misspelling almost every other
word. I told them I lived in a twelve-
by-sixteen foot house way down in the
middle of the woods. I told them I
didn't have any electricity or plumbing
and that I got my drinking water from
a little spring.
    I said I was Northern Michigan's Poet
Laureate. I didn't hear from them for
quite a while after that.

I bought my bugle in Somerville,
New Jersey, along with a bunch of
antiques. I couldn't play it worth
a damn, but one of my goals as a
poet was to teach myself to play taps.

I practiced down at Frog Holler,
in the middle of the woods and the
owls and raccoons. It was pure enjoyment,
surrounded by the trees under the stars,
trying to recapture the call I'd heard
so many years before, while soldiering.

Did I ever tell you about the time
I was raped by a toad? Now a male toad
comes up behind a female toad, and he
strokes her sides with his front legs,
gently causing her to lay eggs. Then
he comes along behind and fertilizes
them. I can't remember where I learned
this ... But I was down by the pond at
Frog Holler one night, enjoying the
stars and the frogs singing, when I
felt this funny rhythm on my foot. I
swung the flashlight down and there
was this toad passionately stroking
my shoe. Jesus! I gave him a little
push into the water.

My paint brush never strays far
from Frog Holler. I'm going to paint
another eight-thousand pictures of
my house, until I've got an even ten-
thousand. Then I'll switch to other
things.

I like it down here at the bottom
of winter. I've watched the hills for

days and noticed how the bare branches
make a delicate crisscross pattern
against the light.

I've worked for hours and hours
trying to capture the greyness after
the sun goes over the hill. And after
a thousand paintings I still haven't
got it. But I'll sell the paintings
for three dollars apiece. I've already
sold a hundred and fifty dollars worth,
and I'm just getting in gear.

Today found me doing little odd
jobs I've neglected for a long time.
For example, adjusting the mirrors
on the trees. I've fastened a couple
rear view mirrors on a tree so I can
keep an eye on my roof and stovepipe
from my rocking-chair at night.

It was an almost endless job.
I'd turn the mirror this way and
that, then come in and sit down.
All I'd have was the sky. But after
much walking and sitting I'm proud
to say they are exact.

Then Ruth, my sister, had some
Christmas lights that wouldn't work.
So I had her give them to me. I don't
have electricity down at Frog Holler
anyway. It won't make any difference.
I hung them all around outside.

Lewis Roy Kirby (my nephew)
and I always kidded each other
about which of us would make
Time magazine first. He was a

cocky kid. He won. His name is
visible on *Time's* first photo of
the Vietnam War memorial.

My youngest grandson took my
old empty shotgun outside to play
and lost it. It laid in the woods
all summer until I finally found
it the other day. Even though it
was all rusted, I took it rabbit
hunting to celebrate. I had to
track down the same rabbit and
shoot it three times before the
gun fired.

This makes the second time Andy,
my youngest son, has introduced me.
The first was for his fourth-grade
class. He ended the introduction
with, "And don't laugh at his beard
either."
After the reciting, he commented
on my poem, *The Giving*. "Dad," he
said, "I didn't like that poem where
you stomped on my sister's face."

Walking out
of Frog Holler
after dark,
we were about
forty yards away
when Max started
blowing taps.
Then he fired

his shotgun up
into the stars,
and all the
tiny pellets
rained down
on us.

    After a stint
of babysitting
up at the house,
Max returned
strutting with
a limp like a
one-man parade,
whistling old
folk tunes into
the dark
to announce
his return,
interrupting all
the younger poets.

    I like it here at Frog Holler,
but I don't want to continue here
forever. The little spring where
I used to get my drinking water,
at night it held the stars ...
They bulldozed it out this summer
enlarging the pond for a golf course.
    Across the lake they silenced
the artesian well with an old towel,
so they could hear my poems better.
That was the end there.
    Last week, while speaking at a
folk festival, I was so weak I
grabbed an aluminum pole holding up

the tent, to stabilize myself. But
the cold in the metal shot right
through me.
   My leg hurt so bad, finally I
just gave up and went home. The next
morning I couldn't get out of bed.
I laid there until early afternoon,
when my body started functioning again.
Old age is not for sissies.

   I made a momentous decision this
week. I've decided to move out of
Frog Holler, into an apartment in
Bellaire. I'll keep my books in the
kitchen cupboard. All I need is my
grandfather clock, my desk and a
couple sleeping bags, plus food.

   I think I had a mild stroke
or something. Standing up there
in front of the kids, I just went
blank. I excused myself and left.
   Now, three days later, I can't
remember what school it was, or
any of my poems. Sometimes I can't
even speak sentences together.
   What a beautiful sunset.
   Florence has been here three or
four times. About the closest to
my words. What I mean.
   Spirits cuddle.

   Max stops his old grandfather clock
   that kept the rhythm of Frog Holler.

*Time is getting on his nerves. A Zen
book of poems lies in the wastebasket,
a cardboard box filling up with wads
of paper and tobacco spit. He sits at
his desk mostly, and sleeps on the
floor.*

*"Max, you should write down these
fragments, your new way of speaking.
They'd make some good Dylan Thomas-
type poems." He grins. "Max, are there
a lot of children sounds around?" Not
enough.*

*Should I tell him everybody in the
restaurant is talking and asking about
him? He always liked to be the center
of attention.*

*The frustration in the room is so
thick you could hit it with a fist.
Max has tried and missed, striking the
lamp above his desk and breaking the
glass.*

So here I am on top the scrap heap
wired for plumbing. Excuse me if I cry
a little. I can't hide my feelings as
easy as I used to. Life is hard and I
guarantee that none of you will get out
of here alive either.

I'm writing a poem about dying.
It'll be called "Fancy Pants," after
these diapers I'm wearing, but you
might have to finish it. If I get
any thinner or weaker, I'm going to
go right through the window.

When I die I'm going to a better
place, and if I don't like it there,
I'm moving on.

*Max could always tell a story
better each time, so he kept
changing them. Now his friends
are arguing about what to do
with his ashes. He told everybody
something different.*

*You get roughly a half gallon
of ashes, depending on the size
of the body. There used to be a
few small bones, but not anymore.
They put them through a grinder
or something. What's left looks
like kitty litter.*

*To solve the problem, Max's sons
buried him in a miniature stone tomb
down at Frog Holler. Then they built
a fire pit over him. Now, every time
you sit around the fire, something
of Max is in the flames.*

*Louan Lechler is the only poet-
singer in the world who wears the
ashes of Max Ellison like a rough
on her face. When they poured him
into the ground, the dust off his
ashes rose and drifted over onto
her.*

Terry Wooten performing at a Stone Circle evening, c. 1988.

Part Five

"Fire is an old story."

– Gary Snyder

Stone Circle

In northern Wisconsin and Minnesota
the Sioux and the Chippewa
still don't get along with each other,
though they both treat rocks with reverence.

There are stones still in earth
just below the surface,
big as prehistoric bulls,
many times stronger
they can break down the biggest tractor
in its tracks.

Pick them up
and place them in a circle,
all the things that rocks have gone through.

The tractor groans,
its steel arms creak,
hydraulic hoses squeal
as I try to levitate
this wild old rock
the modern way
from its nest full of time
and squashed earth.
The stuff this tractor
is made of,
and this ancient old boulder
are like kin,
dust off a star.
In comparison
I'm just a speck in time,
insignificant as an ant
laboring to carry
a sacred egg.　■

Springwells Mound

Just north of where River Rouge pours
into the Detroit River, in the summer
of 1763, the ruins of Springwells Mound
was a mysterious, old, almost sacred
man-made place.

What was left of this Stone Age Renaissance
Center was over four stories high,
500 feet across, and rivaled
the great earthworks of prehistoric
North America.

The Ottawa, Potawatomi and Wyandot
sometimes buried their dead on top.

Way down under, skeletons entombed
for thousands of years lay decorated
in copper hair pipes, amulets, stone jewelry
and shell beads, the grinning skulls
like cornerstones in the old earth
full of secrets.

Chief Pontiac used the place
as a watchtower between the lakes
during his siege of Fort Detroit.

Springwells Mound disappeared piecemeal
for fill dirt for city streets and
miscellaneous landfills. Today, nobody
even knows where it stood.
The bones have blended into the earth,
and scattered under the rumbling steel,
cement and asphalt of Detroit City.   ■

View Site

On top of the Zilwaukee Bridge
the view from the southbound lane
soars over prehistoric Michigan's
most populated region.
The Tittabawassee, Shiawassee, Cass and Flint rivers
and all the tributaries
flow into the Saginaw River delta.
Settlements are old as mammoth bones.

Surveyors in the 1830s
recorded 109 villages, 32 earth mounds,
fifteen burial grounds, a circular enclosure
and one symmetrical garden bed.
In the 1600s Jesuit missionaries
traveling in canoes
chronicled field after field of corn and squash,
among bevies and flocks of wildlife.
Indian trails led out in all directions
from the old downtowns.

As the crow flies north
to the mouth of the Kawkawlin River,
in 1886 on a rise overlooking the water,
stood two large stones
several feet high with flat tops
and a broad base of smaller stones
covered with offerings
of tobacco, pieces of tin and flint.
The sacred boulders
shaped by the glaciers,
were surrounded by giant stumps
and burned timber.   ■

Story of Kewadin

The death of Kewadin, last of the blue-blood
Chippewas, was a time of quiet celebration
among the Christian Indians, and those of the
old ways too. No one knew exactly how old he
was, but it was common knowledge he'd fought
at the Little Bighorn River Massacre on the British side
in 1813. It was the bloodiest battle in Michigan,
at least in modern people's memories. The
little Big Horn pales in comparison. Of the 1,000
U.S. soldiers, only 60 fought their way out,
most of them Kentucky sharpshooters. And old
Kewadin loved telling stories about those who
didn't make it.

After the war the animals seemed to prefer him.
Every spring, he had the biggest belly and the
tallest stack of furs. But like his name, The
Northwest Wind, Kewadin could be just as surly.
In later years people said he went to work for
"Matchi Manitou," an evil spirit who lived on the
dark side of the moon. The Indians of Wequagemog
on the north edge of Elk Lake grew wary of him,
especially his beaver skin pouch full of tricks
and medicine. A patient people, they waited for
the days to sneak up on him one sunrise at a time.

Old Kewadin saw it coming. Two moons before
his death he converted to Christianity and lived
out his days with a smirk, in the sanctuary of
his daughter's home. He died in 1884 surrounded
by winter. They chiseled a grave in the ground
and sent old Kewadin on his way with a bouquet
of dried flowers in one hand and his hunting
knife in the other, plus two extra white shirts
for the long trip through the hunting grounds
to the celestial city. And most important, a long

rope with a grappling hook on the end of it,
to climb over the wall into heaven, in case the
angels refused to let him in. A few years later,
they renamed the town after him. ■

Ghost Crossing

Charlie Bukowski
had been dead for two weeks
before I got the news
while being interviewed
by this woman journalist
who'd stopped smoking cigarettes
after the Harmonic Convergence.

Driving her car home
through the suburbs
into the twilight
just out of the yellow glare
of the city lights;
she hit a shadow of an animal
that really wasn't an animal,
but a spirit or wild green thing
that thumped her bumper,
and ran back into the dark.

She was quitting her job soon
to study under this woman shaman.
She kept having visions,
revelations, chills or something
in the middle of my answers
to her questions.
Once she stared at me so long
with her spiritual headlights
I got nervous.

When Max Ellison was dying,
I know a poet who saw
an apparition of a white rhinoceros
at a ghost crossing on Highway 31
a mile north of our house.
The 45th parallel has a reputation
for these kind of things.
There should be a road sign,
"Caution. Meandering ley line ahead.
Drive slowly and watch out
of your peripheral vision."

After the interview
I felt a little spacy,
so drove down 28th Street
for some secular grounding.
Walking across the parking lot
I whispered to the empty cars
that I couldn't believe
Bukowski was dead.
Then went inside the mall
to watch the pretty girls
for Charlie,
and mourn.   ■

Poem for the Dead Animals Along the Road

Our headlights reflect off shining animal eyes
in the road ahead, so slow the car down.
It's a raccoon jumping into the ditch
the same instant I notice its dead companion
smeared across the pavement by somebody's tires.

Stop the car and get out, but what can I do?
Standing in the road in the dark
a beautiful sad wildness swells over me
under these callous old stars.
Then another car's lights come hissing
over the hill, and scares me away too.

I've been known to roll the window down
and shout warnings to porcupines.
I honk the horn at rabbits and squirrels,
and look out for deer and raccoon.
I'm always picking up painted turtles
and giving them a ride home
since they're my totem.

The other day I rescued one
that'd been flipped like a tiddlywink
out of the southbound lane
onto the shoulder gravel full of fossils.
It was alive,
but had to wait while it peed a puddle
before I put it in the car.
Never once ducked in its shell,
just kept clawing the air and my fingers,
stretching its head and legs way out.
First time I'd ever seen a turtle's
armpits or inner thighs.
Rushed it home to our small pond,
my own personal turtle outpatient
trauma center where it rested in the mud,
then checked out during the night.

The woodlands were here first,
and the animals have been passing
through where these roads are for eons;
muskoxen, mammoths and mastodons,
a huge type of extinct moose,
prehistoric pigs called peccaries,
giant beaver bigger than black bears,

caribou, wolves and big bison
ancestors to the modern buffalo
have all crossed over into dreamtime.
But the painted turtle is still here
and has been for millions of years
like its ornery cousin the snapper.
I keep this all in perspective while driving,
like a cave painting inside my head.
I'm old fashioned. I respect my elders
and their smallish descendants.   ■

Coyote's Back

Coyote's back
and you guys are gonna be sorry.
Hey la, hey la,
coyote's back.
He's kind of big for his size
and he's awful strong and scrawny.
Hey la, hey la,
coyote's back.

Every time a rabbit disappears
or a fawn comes up missing
you blame coyote.
Ooowh, ooowh.
You guys have been saying things
about him that really aren't true.
Ooowh.
So look out now,
cuzz coyotes are pretty tough cookies.
You'd better watch out for your poodles.

Hey la, hey la,
coyote's back.   ■

Nothing Happened Happy Today

(For Blaise)

Nothing happened happy today.
I don't want to go to bed.
I'd rather stand, stomp and scream
and throw a fit instead.
They miscounted my library books.
Don't know where my free ice-cream coupon's at.
My baseball team got beat 23 to 6
and I didn't even get a chance to bat.
I had to go to the bathroom
during the last two innings.
Coach kept yelling, "Stay awake out there!"
That's why I wasn't grinning.
I had to grit my teeth and hold it
all the way to the grocery store.
Then my seashell necklace broke
and spilled all over Grandma's floor.
Nothing happened happy today.
I'm awful tired and sad.
Now Daddy's writing this poem.
I don't know whether to giggle or be mad.   ■

Silhouette

Jack Kerouac's ghost
made it to Stone Circle,
but wouldn't enter the ring.
It was an older burnt-out Kerouac
who didn't believe
in Dharma anymore,
and didn't want to talk about it.
Too much booze and speed
mixed in with the beat,

like a worn out soul
from crisscrossing America,
the awful, growling, sprawling cities
and all the little towns
sprinkled under infinity.
He lurked in the shadows,
leaning up against a car,
smoking cigarettes under the stars
and sulking about time
like a sad, human angel
who'd seen too much
and sacrificed himself
for a few great novels and poems.
I didn't approach him.
I sensed he wanted to be alone
way-out on the edge
of this poetry mandala
made of billion-year-old stones,
where you can hear the images
rippling out like wishes
through people's heads,
into the unfathomable universe
inside and outside of us.   ■

The Bob Dylan Disease

Back in the 1960s
I would have figured you
had the Bob Dylan Disease.
Some bad cases could be terminal,
and there wasn't any one symptom.
I lost two friends from it.

One just wasted away
sulking on the couch,
smoking toilet paper

in his overnight jail cell,
hiding from things
that go wrong in life
with his stereo
loud as it would go,
blowing his harmonica
to Bob's tunes.
He passed on out of my life
from lack of personal inspiration.

The other led the only protest
march I was ever in.
A year later he was committed
to a state insane asylum.
I knew he was in trouble
when he said it was hard
living life according to Dylan.
He blew a fuse one night
in the Crossroads Restaurant.
After that I stopped
following leaders,
and rebelled more subtly.
But I still listen to Bob's songs.
I don't blame him.

It's all right if you don't
want to work on "Maggie's Farm,"
but you don't want to work period.
You're just using art
and various causes
as an excuse.
Sometimes it's hard
living up to your dreams,
especially when
you have such good ones.
Trouble is you're sleepwalking
through the physical plane,
and your life has become a nightmare
for your real friends.   ■

I'm a Mom (For Kelly)

Now when I was a little girl
About the age of five
I had something in my 'magination
Keep a lot of folks alive

Now I'm a woman
Just passed 21
With two little babies
A lot of work and a lot of fun

I'm a Mom
Spelled M O M   Mom

All my pretty babies (husband included)
Stand in line
I can love you all
For hours at a time

I'm a Mom
Spelled M O M   Mom

I'm goin' back home
To Michigan next summer
Bring back my husband lover
John the poet-conqueror

I'm a Mom
Spelled M O M   Mom

The looks I shoot
Will never miss
The way I love 'em
They can't resist

I'm a Mom
Spelled M O M   Mom   ∎

Ode to Ernie Harwell

Over 5,000 Detroit Tiger ballgames ago,
Grandpa took me trout fishing
on the Butterfield Creek.
On the way home half asleep
I listened to Ernie Harwell
recite the late innings
of a Tiger ballgame
while Grandpa's cigarette glowed
like a campfire in the dark.
Outside the car windows
Michigan flowed along.
I felt content as a young trout
snuggled under a log in the current.

Since that night
only thing on the radio
that's rivaled rock 'n' roll
(or country and western music)
is Ernie Harwell going on and on
like an epic poem full of Ty Cobb
trivia and Detroit Tiger history,
like a human baseball encyclopedia
always sounding the same,
but always different
through three decades and most
of the incarnations of my life.
I even proposed to my wife with
Ernie crooning in the background,
or was it the Rolling Stones'
song, "Time Waits for No One"?

That was over 2,000 Tiger games ago.
Grandpa's been gone since 1979.
Late that last September he whispered,
"Psst, I've got a secret, I'm dying."
Then he sat there like an old house
beside the road and watched life go by
like a Denny McClain fastball.

There isn't any real security,
but Ernie Harwell on the airwaves
came close.   ■

November

The famous leaves have blown off.
I'm standing in a parking lot
off the freeway,
watching the sunrise
over Osceola County.
It's a purple dawn
with stars glittering
like frost on God's windshield.
The horizon rim is blaze orange.
Next week is firearms deer season.
Death and deer are tiptoeing
through the noisy leaves.
The colors are shadows of browns,
greys and hang tough greens.
Weak sunrays slant a golden haze
through bare trees.
I was born in November.
The sights and smells
set off primal memories.
My nose gets sentimental
over the cold and decaying,
or it could be allergies.   ■

Winn Edwards' Deer Hunting Poem

Prologue
"When are you going to write
that deer hunting poem about us?
We're not getting any younger you know.
We don't have many deer seasons left.
Takes a lot of luck to get this old.
Don't wait until we're dead and gone
and can't read it, when we're just
memories like old antlers."

Grandma says,
"Men are taken by
a kind of fever
at this time of year.
When they're not deer hunting
all they do is talk about it
around the kitchen table.
They gossip over every move
the deer make.
The poor deer
don't have any privacy.
Winn Edwards is worst of all.
Often times I just turn down
my hearing aid,
but the other day
I overheard him say that he's in love
with this one pretty doe
and what he wouldn't give
to be hers for a while.
That's going a little too far
if you ask me.
He's a good, decent man,
but I think he's killed and ate
so many bucks
they're coming alive inside of him,
making him say crazy things.
Maybe I'm getting too sentimental

in my old age,
because it's as if
they worship the deer
in a strange old way,
though they'd never openly admit it,
and most people wouldn't
understand anyway.
Still, it bothers me,
how on Sundays the church bells
are sandwiched between
rifle shots echoing."   ∎

Lake Superior Storm

The waves are a scary, pretty, turquoise blue;
the violent lightning flashing on and off
like a jagged light bulb. It's a wild party of white caps
with huge waves crashing against the rocks
like the beating of drums. Boom! Boom! The big
beautiful, white waves thundering everywhere
against the break wall. Excited schools of fish
struggling to stay in the clean, angry water
swishing back and forth, roaring in the storm
like a wild spirit flying up out of the water,
like a laughing giant polishing the cliffs!
Gallant, marvelous waves pulverizing themselves
against the oldest rocks in the world. Splashing,
smashing, roaring, scary, blue Lake Superior!
Woe to anyone caught out on it.

Later, as nature calms itself and the sunlight shines,
the sturgeon and seagulls come out from hiding.   ∎

Teaching Is a Tough Business

Standing in front of the class
trying to teach William Faulkner's
short story, "The Bear,"
she was overcome by the imagery;
the doomed forest almost a hundred
miles deep, the mangled claw legend
big as twenty years of stories,
the baying hounds verging on hysteria,
trying to chase a beast that wouldn't run,
just moseyed along like some bored God,
the old Indian who worshipped the Bear,
the boy-man who learned to surrender
to the woods almost as old as the earth,
to leave behind his rifle, his compass
and finally even his Grandfather's watch
and walk in intersecting circles
deep in the sun-sprinkled greenish
grey browns of the ancient forest,
the little mongrel dog whose bravery
sounded like a mad squeaky toy.

Standing in front of the class
she was overcome by the sadness
of a few kids just not interested
in knowing anything about Faulkner,
or any writer for that matter.
She started crying quiet, shy tears
down her cheeks like leaky feelings.
Finally, that got the kids' interest.   ■

Saint Francis Would Be Proud

There was a cashier's window
at this Christian college,
and winter semester's tuition was due
before Christmas break.
Just outside the window
on a bulletin board in the hallway,
was a poster about giving
to needy and homeless people.
The poster was a collage
of sad, color photos
to stress the issue.

The cashier's window was doing a good business.
Everything was running smoothly,
until one eighteen-year-old student
had a religious experience
standing in line beside the poster
advertisement for the poor.
He signed over his tuition check,
his parents' money
and his Grandma's loan,
to the clerk for the homeless;
figuring God would take care of him,
since He always had.

An hysterical mom and dad flew in
and gave a secular sermon
full of capitalistic dogma
to the dean to the effect
that if the university
was going to encourage such compassion,
it had to accept responsibility
when pure moments
like this happened.

The university reluctantly agreed.
The poor and homeless were left out
in the same old harmony.
Now everything is back on self-center.
The eighteen-year-old student
is spiritually and academically
focused straight ahead.
But for one sublime afternoon
another human being knew
what it meant
to really mean it.   ■

Winter Solstice Rabbit

I heard the rifle crack three times
as the rabbit darted
from under the brush,
and zig-zagged through the wild grass
into the swamp.
Focusing through the thicket
I spotted it dying,
thrashing in the snow.
Balancing on top of the brush pile
I pointed my son
to his first kill.

Death isn't a small thing
even to a rabbit,
especially to a thirteen-year-old boy-man
standing over it
with an old 22 semi-automatic rifle,
a gift from my dead uncle
when I was a boy.

After the last breath
Ezra carried it out of the woods

to where I was waiting.
The great mystery settled in
calming the rabbit.
My son's lips quivered
as he declined
trying for another kill.

Walking back to the house
the young hunter
carried rabbit and rifle,
and a new responsibility
old as the sacred cave paintings.
Mom took pictures with her camera,
a modern family ritual
so we'll remember in twenty years.
Then we cleaned it for dinner
to celebrate now.   ■

Night Watch

There's a real bogeyman loose tonight.
Police bulletins
are flashing across the TV.
Outside the icy windows
it's five below zero
with icy moonlight
reflecting off the snow.

A Special Report
says he escaped from jail,
hurt a mother, scared her kids
and kicked them out of their car.
He left two bachelor brothers dead in a house,
took their deer rifles,
boxes of ammunition
and a blood-red colored car.

He robbed an old lady
and locked her in her closet.
Now he's coming our way.

Police bulletins
say keep your door locked.
Our kids are afraid to go to bed.
My son thinks he hears him
on the porch roof
scratching at his bedroom window.
My daughter is huddled under
her covers shivering.
Dad's a brave face,
but downstairs I've got the shotgun ready.
It's a bad night to turn the other cheek
or despise his crimes inside me.
Got to be a father first.
The two men he killed are forever
and the stars aren't interested.

After our kids are finally asleep,
a pair of headlights
ease up our dead-end road
stopping out front.

My heartbeats are a stampede.
Using the moon for a flashlight
I can see silhouettes
of two men in a pickup,
part of a posse or the bogyman's
got a hostage with a truck.
As the headlights arc around
back towards the highway,
I let the dogs out
to be sure they're gone.
I rest all night on the couch
with my shotgun for a Teddy Bear.   ■

My Favorite Critic

My sixth-grade daughter complains
that I measure the world
too much with poetry.
We'll be talking
about hippies, the plague,
Michigan History or the Civil War …
I'll mention some poet
in relation to the times …
She'll groan
and stomp out of the room.
In schools I wouldn't
have to take this.
She'd be sent
to the principal's office.
At home I sit flabbergasted
on the couch
while she storms up the stairs
to her room
like some feminine tornado
slamming the door against poetry.
But at least she knows
who Jack Kerouac was
whether she wants to
or not.   ■

This Is Better Than Meditation

The rain and the frogs singing
under an invisible full moon
were more interesting
than the 11 o'clock news.
Turned the porch light on.
Night crawlers were partying,

thousands of them
crawling all over
the cement and driveway,
getting it on,
braiding themselves in the grass.
I couldn't resist.
I put my raincoat on,
grabbed my flashlight
and waded out into the primitive.

Humming along with the frogs
it's all come back to this.
Hunched over in the dark
with a flashlight,
sneaking up on night crawlers,
pouncing on them
stretched out in the rain.
I can feel their bodies recoil
like slippery nerves pulling back
quick into the wet earth.
My muddy fingers are strong
and know just where to pinch,
but I miss half of them.

Night crawlers didn't live in our yard
when I was a kid at home.
Dad would drive us
to the cemetery west of town
to catch the giant worms
in the dark warm rain.
We'd hunt through the old and new graves
with our flashlights
like absentminded will-o'-the-wisps
gathering night crawlers
in big coffee cans.
Later we'd trade them to the river
and lakes for fish.
I didn't realize how rich
we were then.   ■

Stars and Eternity

Every poem I write lately
ends with some image
about stars and eternity.
I'm in a spiraling rut.
I wax sappy and sentimental
under the Milky Way.
How can one not be aware
of the vastness
and smallness of life
just by looking up and out
on a clear night?
Oh, how the people
under the street lights
suffer without knowing it.
Stars and eternity
keep breaking out
like cosmic acne
in the middle of my poems.
For example,
these callous old stars,
immortal old stars,
under the sparkling dark,
stars brace themselves,
the seed I planted is still
small as a star,
frogs start singing again,
the stars look like their voices.
Got drunk
and tap danced on a piece of plywood
for the stars.
See what I mean.
If it wasn't for the stars and eternity
I wouldn't have to lie awake
nights on the couch
under the picture window
worrying about money and gravity,
admiring the meteors.

Every poem I write lately
ends with some image
about stars and eternity.
I'm in a spiraling rut.   ■

What's Wrong With You!

Every time I mow a lawn I think of Walt
Whitman's *Leaves of Grass* and start to
feel silly, so I let my poetic mind loaf.
But I backed over Great-Grandma's dahlias
with the riding lawn mower, cutting
weeds along the side of the garage.
I admit I noticed a white flower collapse
under a blur of chopping knife blades
and popping pistons. It just didn't
consciously register, until later,
when I returned from coffee break.
Great-Grandma came charging out of
her house shaking her cane angrily.
"What's wrong with you!" she scolded.
"You're a poet! Poets are supposed to
love flowers, not mow them down!"
I'm sort of a sensitive guy. After
about two minutes of verbal abuse
Great-Grandma hurt my feelings.
I almost sassed back some poetic
lame excuse, but decided against it.
Great-Grandma had 50 years of seniority
over me. Her cane was making me nervous.
So I just stood there with my head down,
feeling ashamed, watching her angry cane
out of the corner of my eye, like some
condemned poetic warrior.   ■

Garage Sale

Great-Grandma doesn't live
in her red brick house anymore.
She's been moved to an old folk's home.
But her fluorescent yellow irises
are in full bloom, and I still mow
her lawn. At dusk in mid-July
a new generation of hummingbird moths
flock around the flowers as if drawn
by the yellow glow as much as the nectar.
I mow carefully beside them.
The last afternoon Great-Grandma visited
the rooms where she'd lived for sixty years,
I stopped in. It was my turn to check on her,
but words were a broken washing machine.
This Fourth of July picnic Great-Grandma
couldn't recognize us, only Torch Lake.
She kept hoping her husband,
who's been dead for five years,
would show up soon, because
she didn't know any of these people.
She's closer to her dead friends now
than living family. I wish I could
taste senility like a hummingbird moth
does this nectar, then return
and remember what it's like.
Instead, I took my pick of her books
like Great-Grandma once said I could,
before they emptied the shelves.
I painted the white trim and helped
reroof the house so they can sell it.
Now all that's left to do is mow
around the For Sale sign
and get ready for the garage sale.　■

Fame

Drove into the gas station
in my mini poetry-pickup,
and steered around two burly guys
talking and smoking cigarettes
and blocking the drive
with their tough 4 X 4 trucks.

I didn't like how they were dominating
the place.
My mood simmered like the gas fumes.
Filled up
and went inside to pay.

"How's the poetry business?"
the girl behind the cash register
asked me.
"Good," I answered,
"if those idiots out front
don't blow me up
smoking cigarettes."

The girl went outside
and made the men put their ciggies out.
I felt like a tattletale.

"HEY! GET A JOB!"
the biggest guy yelled at me,
as I hurried out
past the pumps
to my pickup.
I was mildly flattered and intimidated.
They recognized me too!
"I GOT ONE!"
I shouted back
safe inside my cab.
"NO YOU DON'T!"
he shot back.

This was the critical moment,
but couldn't think of anything
intelligent to say.
Didn't have much
to bounce off of.
Wish I'd taken debate in high school.
I could've put him down,
but there was no sense
in getting beat up.

Sneered over my shoulder,
and drove away
to write a poem.
It'll last longer
than a black eye or bruises.   ■

You're Up!

A jagged lightning storm,
a silver curtain of rain
delayed the softball game
for two hours.
By 7:30 the girls were
charged up with chocolate
and playing ball around mud puddles.
In the middle of a soggy third inning
a double rainbow lit up
over the east.
Sassy Sally was pitching
and stopped to look up
above the bleachers
full of noisy parents.
Rosie was hanging sideways
from the rafters in the dugout.
The cheers rippled out
like exploding wishes.

"Hey, batter, batter!
Hey, batter, batter!"
"Can I play shortstop?"
"I want to play batter!"
"Where's third?"
"Where's my glove?"
"Where's a ball?"
"Can I pitch?"
"Who's the next batter?
"How come I have to sit out?"
"I only batted once last game."
"Where's my hat?"
"Swing hard ya retard!"
"Girls!
I don't want to hear
anymore of that!"

A hundred years from now
these girls and us parents
will be mostly forgotten
like anonymous photographs
that haunt our attics.
But right now
the most important thing is
who are the first three batters
of the next inning.   ■

The "P" Word

"I'll bet you're going to write
a poem about this,"
people are always saying.
Or they'll suggest,
"There must be a poem here,"

and motion around
into thin air
at what's happening.

They're right.
I can feel it.
I'm just not ambitious enough
or prolific enough
to write them all.
I write as an excuse
to loaf and observe time
in a ritual of consciousness.

Then there are the iron men
neighbors afraid of the "P" word.
We'll be talking
about deer hunting,
sports or the weather.
They'll start to ask
if I'm still doing my _____?
An embarrassed expression
will blush over their faces
and start squirming around.

I let us off the hook.
I answer, "Yes,
I'm still writing,"
but don't mention the "P" word.
Then quickly change the subject.

She commented after my workshop,
"You're a lot better
than those professor poets.
You're not as intelligent."
Her friend followed,
her eyes rolling
and said,
"I think she means intellectual." ■

After A Bad Audience

I want to work
in a lumber yard
stacking boards
and 2 by 4s.
I want to run up
to a pickup
and say,
"Can I help you sir?"

I'm sick of this
poetry business,
always looking, listening
for the next idea
to write about
and prove
I can still do it.

I want to build up
some calluses
on these soft pink palms.
Maybe cut off
a finger or thumb
on a table saw,
so I look tougher
when those younger poets
come around.

I'm tired
of polishing poems
in motels and hotels.
I'm worn out
from 500 thousand miles
on the road.

I want to retire
in a lumber yard
close by every day.

I love sawdust,
the smell of it,
taste and feel of it.

Trouble is
I like trees,
monarch butterflies
and spotted owls better.
And I hate lifting
bundles of roofing
and 50-pound bags of cement.　　■

Empty Wallet

I need to buy something.
I haven't bought anything in months.
A camouflaged raincoat,
a Doors CD,
fifty feet of rope,
some new material possession
to keep my mind off poetry.
I'm metaphorically constipated
and bored sitting at my desk
trying to follow my bliss,
and memorizing Chaucer's
"Complaint to His Empty Purse."

Reading the shoppers guide
I see they're having a big tarp sale
in my hometown.
I can't take it anymore.
I'm going to drive to the mall
and walk around window shopping.
I don't care if any
if my friend see me.
But how come there's no poetry section
in the mall bookstores?　　■

Mimi

Mimi rides the merry-go-round
night after night
bored with the smiling horses.
She sits in the chair with her winter coat on
in late summer.
Mimi's not too clean.
Her hair hangs in wind braids
like tangled dreams.
And she's tired
and wants to go home,
wherever that is,
or the carnival's heading.
But her mama is too busy
selling tickets,
and her grandpa is too busy
giving rides
and smoking his pipe.
So Mimi rides the merry-go-round
night after night
bored with the smiling horses.   ■

For Kate

Mrs. Murphy exited to the office,
trusting her class
for just a minute.
A fair, willowish, fifth-grade girl
with long, bouncing, blond hair
pranced to the front of the class
with four doo-wopping friends.

Kate had memorized my *Mimi* poem
without her teacher knowing.
She turned it into a Motown song,
and practiced all week
in front of her mirror
and at a friend's house.

The go-go girl sang my lines,
swiveling her hands and hips
like a wobbling top.
Her backup chorus
shuffled to-and-fro
crooning, "Mimi, Mimi, Mimi."

Mrs. Murphy returned in the middle
of a standing ovation.
Encore!
Kate took my poem to a higher level.
When I visited her school
a week later
Kate performed for me.

Almost two years down the road
I was in a hotel room with a view
of an intersection
on a rainy January day.
My wife telephoned.
Mrs. Murphy wanted me to know
a vicious strain of leukemia
had snuffed Kate Lauren Heinrich's
bright life out.
Her seventh-grade friends sang
my remodeled poem as a eulogy
in celebration of her life.

I've got a funeral program,
pictures of a fifth-grade Kate,
and another of a blossoming young woman

with short blond hair
and a firm smile.
November 1st is still her birthday.

When the muse doesn't move me,
my left knee aches,
or the sharks of cynicism are circling ...
I think of Kate
and keep going.   ∎

Carnival Ponies

The Oglala holy man said,
"All things in their greatest power
move in circles."
He never saw these carnival ponies
with their halters chained
from both sides
to a steel yoke rotating around.
The little ponies walk in circles
through time
with their heads down.
Each week
they stare at a different rut
in the ground,
barely noticing the children
standing in line to pay a dollar
to ride them.
After dark
Grandma Wallenda sways back and forth
on a pole reaching almost to heaven,
flirting with her ancestors
while the people gasp and clap.

The little ponies shift
from hoof to hoof

waiting to be let loose,
for a drink
or some hay or grain,
as the two men who own them
count their money. ■

"Let the Frog Loose!"

I'm not proud of this,
but as a boy
I used to do frightful things to frogs.
As a grown man
I have lots of ghastly frog ghosts
in my subconscious.
They're the skeleton keys
to my environmentalism.

I don't eat frog legs anymore.
I'd rather listen to them sing.
I treat frogs with a special
reborn kind of gentleness.
In the spring
they're like little green summer soldiers
with songs for weapons
to conquer winter away.

In the countryside where I live
the early summer nights vibrate
with frogs chirping.
I like to stand outside in the sparkling dark
and just listen.

She told me as a child
she used to have nightmares
about a six-foot-tall frog
somebody kept in a cage.

At five o'clock on a summer afternoon
every now and then
somebody would yell,
"Let the frog loose!"

Everybody would run and hide
so the six-foot frog
wouldn't get them.
But she could never find a place
to hide fast enough.
A six-foot frog would always catch her
in the middle of the street,
and jump on her
and lick her.   ■

Hawk's Eulogy

The kids outgrew our big, smelly, old black dog
with the giant mole on his lip
and gross, pear-shaped hemorrhoid
on his other end.
They forgot how he ran between them
with their tiny hands in his mouth,
and the tag games
around the kitchen table.

Hawk had a skin condition
that got worse as he grew older.
It oozed up through his dreaded locks
that never quit growing.
Sand and grass stuck to him.
It dulled two pair of shears
to cut his hair.
You couldn't pet him
without absorbing bad body odor.

The dog had a big, dumb heart
and soft porcupine brown eyes
the opposite of his name.
When he got mad or scared
he'd grin through his crooked teeth.
Other than chasing cars
turning around in our driveway,
Hawk learned one trick,
how to shake hands,
and practiced it his whole life.
He didn't chase deer,
he followed them as they browsed along.

Hawk was somewhat of a mystic
his last two years.
It was like the old dog saw
into another dimension,
a parallel world.
He'd stand and stare into space
and bark and bark and bark at things
the rest of us couldn't see.
This totally puzzled the beagle
who had a very practical nose.

I backed over Hawk by accident
while he was sleeping
under my poetry pickup.
I had to put him down
in the driveway
beside a lilac bush in full bloom.
I was afraid he wouldn't stop dying,
but he did like the good dog
he always was.
I dug a hole swarmed by mosquitoes
in 90-degree humidity,
and buried him under a flat rock for a tomb
before the kids got home
from the last day of school.   ■

Ghost in the Loom

Miss Maude Freeman never married.
She ran a little grocery store
along the D.T.I. Railroad
in Chillicothe, Ohio.
She liked hiring kids
to have them around and to help.
Neighbors all called her Aunt Maude.

A hundred years after Tecumseh died
fighting to keep the Shawnee land,
Henry Ford would stop by
in his private Pullman car.
The whole neighborhood would
take a break to see him
give all the children nickels.
Aunt Maude drove touring Buicks.
She bought a loom at Sears and Roebucks,
and wove rag rugs while tending store.

An 81-year-old niece can remember
standing on packing crates
to slice cheese and chewing tobacco
amid the clutter of antique smells.
One odd boy murdered Aunt Maude
for money in her purse and till.
People said her spirit
hid inside the loom to sulk.

The niece inherited the loom,
and later sold it to a school librarian
up in Flint, Michigan.
Since Aunt Maude liked kids,
she kept her in the media center
of Swartz Creek Middle School,
until she retired.

"Be careful, it's haunted,"
she told me after we'd loaded the loom
out of her garage into my pickup.
"Last person to ever warp it
was Aunt Maude, and she was stabbed.
I paid for the loom,
but I want you and your wife to have it."
She handed me an envelope.
"Read this, I wrote down its history."

Driving out of Flint
I could feel the weight of superstition
like a big load in the back of my pickup.
Drove cautious until I crossed
the Zilwaukee Bridge.
North of Standish where trees thicken
and the earth rises steadily
out of the old glacial depression,
Aunt Maude's ghost lightened up. ■

Earth Day

All Earth Day I kept remembering
the Vietnam War Moratorium Day,
and the millionaire's son's defiant boast,
"I don't want the war to end!
I own war stocks!"

He told me this
after I asked him for the day off.

Then he leaned back in his desk chair,
smirked and folded his hands
behind his head
like an inside out prayer,

and asked me and the world
what we thought of that.

All Earth Day was one big deja vu
of a nineteen-year-old's frustration
standing before him.
The poems, songs and pledges
were anthems in another war
against his kind of thinking.　　■

Drum

I've got an imaginary shaman's drum
made of a warrior's skin and bones,
and I worship the polluted lakes and rivers.

Surfing the semis,
riding the oil-stained
asphalt and cement wave
of the late 20th Century
bumping down a worn out freeway.

Looking across the water
at a shoreline that used to be solid trees,
all I can see are new houses,
strip malls, golf courses and casinos.

So I don't get too depressed
I keep reminding myself
we're living between the glaciers.
Then all this development
for quick money
is just a blip in eternity.

It puts life back into focus
like Bob Marley sang,
"Cuzz none of them can stop the time."　　■

Unfinished Business

The third night
after Grandpa Wooten's death,
I woke up hugging a celestial body
of twilight swarming above me.

I gasped a breath to myself
and fainted back to sleep
in a shawl of raw meat
and sweat of understanding.

Next day was Grandpa's funeral,
but I didn't go.
I was twenty-two years old
and wrote a poem as an excuse.

For years those arrogant lines
have haunted me.
They don't acknowledge ancestral memories
and genetic gifts
I'm now realizing.

October 1971,
the Vietnam War and Peace Movement
had turned into a civil war
inside us.
The 1960s were skidding into the '70s
like a collision.
It was dangerous
traveling rural America
wearing long hair like a peace sign,
and I didn't have a car.
Those are my excuses.

In spirit
I've returned to make amends.
I exhume Grandpa's bones,
clean, polish and powder them.

I apologize
and wrap him into a spirit bundle
shaped like a frontal pack.
I carry Grandpa's skeleton
to a reburial
in a little spirit house
place inside my heart.　　■

Turn Here

Chaucer has been dead for 600 years,
and doesn't remember
he was a great medieval poet.
The atoms that composed him
have gathered for a reunion,
a constellation in a semi-truck driver
with a regular route crossing
northern lower Michigan and the U.P.
Geoffrey still has a faint interest in poetry,
though mostly through his wife
who belongs to a local writing group.
His lady of twenty-eight years has been pestering him
to take her to an outdoor poetry gathering
where people sit in a circle on boulders
and say poems around a fire.
It sounds a little weird to him,
but he knows where it is.
He passes the road signs
every Friday on his way home.
Last week humming south in his eighteen-wheeler,
under a purple and orange sunset
in a good overdrive mood,
Geoffrey blasted his cosmic horn
as he stormed by like a comet.
Interrupting the poets made him chuckle.
Geoffrey has been dead for 600 years,
but still has that great sense of humor.　　■

Why I Dance With My Hands in My Pockets

I hate these dollar dances
at wedding receptions.
I never know what to say
to the young bride.
I want to warn her about
the great doubts that swell over love,
like boring grey clouds,
and tell her to hang tough,
but I just smile
and say, "Congratulations."
I want to enlighten the shining young bride
to the 12th Century troubadour poets
who rebelled against the Church,
medieval tradition
and arranged marriages
to explore the psychology of love,
the spiritualism of the spark
when eyes meet,
about having faith in your own experiences.
Instead I ask,
"Where are you going on your honeymoon?"
I almost tell her
about the overwhelming humility
I felt at the birth of my kids,
the power of vulnerability,
but I don't want to sound
like some sentimental old fart.
Besides, my time is up.
Another man is tapping at my shoulder,
so I just say,
"Good Luck."   ■

Roethke's Historical Marker Dedication

The Presbyterian minister
said he was a bit nervous
in the presence of so many poets.
At the cemetery
for the invocation
over the grave,
Reverend gave a little too much oomph
during "The Saginaw Song".
He conjured up Roethke's spirit
by accident.
The manic depressive Michigan weather
was bad enough.
The wind got colder
and it started raining bigger drops.

I rode back to Roethke's house
with the pretty carnation lady
in her van full of dog hair.
Thunder grumbled over Gratiot Avenue.
There was some faint lightning
that everybody ignored.
It rained on
the political speeches,
students reading their poems
and the marker dedication.
To squeeze around the audience
people were stepping through the crocuses
on their way to the podium.
I stood on the front steps
with the host and her daughter
under an umbrella.

The Saginaw Police closed off the street
and detoured traffic
through the neighborhood

where the greenhouses once stood.
Semis couldn't make the tight turns,
so the traffic cops
let the trucks pass.
A beer truck rattled by.
Ted's ghost was perched on top
with a brew in his left hand
toasting the event.
Only three poets saw him.
Two cousins;
Don, dressed in a leaf-green blazer
and bent like a stem over his cane,
and smiling Mary Ellen
unveiled the historical marker
to all shapes of applause.

I was the after-dinner speaker,
but didn't mention
Ted's apparition.   ∎

Yard Lights

Our new neighbors from the suburbs
have installed
two powerful twin-beam yard lights
on their vacation house;
his hunting cabin
and her suburban outpost.

He's a builder
making big money
on urban sprawl.

We were the only house
on top of the hill
at the end of the road.

For seventeen years
we used a 75-watt bulb
for a yard light
to keep the universe at bay.

If the northern lights were out
we turned our light bulb off.

Our neighbors are up
for the weekend.
Tonight the meadow down the hill
looks like a prison yard.
Four overbearing beams of light
blare out
through the trees.
Morel mushrooms have stopped growing,
and night crawlers are confused.

Yesterday my new neighbor
asked me
if there were any bears around.
"Just the Big Dipper," I lied.
But he can't see the night sky
from his yard.

I can't wait
till the leaves grow bigger
and the bugs come out.   ■

To Wendi for Our 25th Anniversary

(Sept. 20)

I was trimming the roofing
on the Poem Dome
with a sharp utility knife.
You sauntered down
in your loose blouse
to see how I was doing.

The nurse at the Emergency Center
preparing my left thumb
for eight stitches,
said I was a lucky man
if I could still be that distracted
by my wife
after twenty-five years.

When I was young
I proposed to girls
like some guys dip for smelt.
When I proposed to you,
you turned the net on me
and I got lucky.

I like your peaches
and cherry pies.
I like your sugar pears.
I like how you tease flowers
and treat me nice.
I like how you pet
your dead grandma's lonely tom cat.
To be continued.   ∎

Lonesome (For Bethany, the youngest daughter)

Sophie lost her first fiancé
in a car accident.
She almost died with him,
but returned to herself
in the hospital.
A priest was giving her last rites.
"Would you be quiet," she said,
"I'm trying to rest."

Sophie was a city girl from Flint.
Joke was her dad owned a grocery store
in the red light district.
A second generation Serbian,
she met Chuck Shinn at
a Young Communists gathering.
The late '30s was an idealistic time,
troubled like the '60s,
with revolution and utopia in the air.
They were good years to be young
and full of the future.
Sophie was drawn to Chuck's sincerity
and great big handshake.

They moved up north
back to his family farm
to live Thomas Jefferson's vision
of an agrarian society.

Three baby girls later Sophie stumbled
carrying a broom and laundry basket
down a stairway.
Before she caught her balance
the broom handle
poked her in the eye socket.
The young wife didn't dwell on her bruise.
There was too much to do.

Next morning Sophie got out of bed,
teasing Chuck.
It was his turn to cover the fussing baby.
She paused and fell
like a heavy blanket.
Autopsy said
she was gone before she touched the floor,
from a hemorrhaging blood vessel
in her brain.

Chuck moved back to Flint
where Sophie was buried.
He raised their daughters,
and carried on.
Chuck never remarried,
and was always shy
around the light of a woman's body.   ∎

Legend

During the Joe McCarthy era
in the 1950s,
the auto plant bosses where Chuck worked
found out
from company spies
that Chuck was one of the original unionizers
and sit-down strikers
in the 1930s.

Company thugs roughed him up.
An old front page photo
in *The Flint Journal*
showed Chuck being dragged out
of the factory door
with his shirt half torn off.

Chuck was beat-up
and hung upside down by his ankles
from an eight-story window
in downtown Flint.

The thugs told him
if he came back to work,
next time
they'd drop him on his head
to the sidewalk below.

Chuck gave his three little girls
to his close friends,
poet Max Ellison and his wife Florence
for protection.

He went back to work.　　■

Bethany's Story

My sisters and I were pretty young
when we stayed with Max and Florence.
We didn't know why.
Dad would come home beat-up a lot,
and there was a scary feeling
in our own house.

The two things I remember most
were the spying car
always parked down the road,
and the bad storm
we had one night.

Florence was away somewhere,
and tornado warnings
were all over the radio.

Us kids ran in
where Max was writing
at the kitchen table
and whined,
"But if a tornado comes where will we go?"
Max just smiled and pointed up.
Somehow it made us all feel safer.   ■

Troublemaker

At 82 years old
Chuck Shinn
was still on the Michigan State Police
troublemakers list.
It was his Flint unionizing days
in the 1930s,
being a socialist
during The Great Depression.

As the new millennium approached
like an 80-miles-per-hour parade
of material possessions
headed north
out of the cities
for the weekend,
Chuck's stubborn simplicity held true
like a good compass
nobody used anymore.

Everywhere he went
the ghosts of Ben Franklin,
Thomas Jefferson
and Joe Hill
traveled along urging,
"Give 'em heck Chuck!
Give 'em heck!"

Chuck was raised a Mennonite
and never could swear very well.

He spent his teen years hoboing
across Woody Guthrie's vision
of our land,
and worked
for the Civilian Conservation Corps
planting white pines
to repair what the lumber barons did.
The tops of those trees
were his favorite steeple.

At the end of his life
and the 20th Century
Chuck believed in
goodness and honesty
for their own sake,
and made no apologies.   ■

The Road I Wish He'd Not Taken
(Apologies to Robert Frost)

Whose gravel road this is
I don't think he knows.
Our house is on the hill though.
We can't see him stopping here
to pee in the middle
of Stone Circle Drive.
He gives his little horse a shake
and speeds away.

People have been desecrating
our road randomly for years,
but this guy is like clockwork.
Pee spots with bull's-eye washouts

began appearing mysteriously
in January 2001.
Like crop circles
they continue.

Before I peed on somebody's road
I'd want to know
what I was letting out
or holding in,
and to whom I was like to give offence.
Something there is that doesn't love
a stranger peeing every morning
on our road.
My elfish side resents his routine.

It's his regularity that bothers me,
and the yellow spots
gleam so arrogant
in fresh snow and gravel.
I walk this road practicing poems.
Our neighbor lady strolls here
with her baby.
He could at least pee in the ditch,
if he has miles to go before he rest,
and miles to go before he rests.   ■

The Crossing

Driving along another development road
through the wetlands off Lake Michigan,
I saw a big doe
and her brand new fawn
crossing in front
of my poetry truck windshield.
They weren't in any hurry
and neither was I.

Something invisible
and older than love
connected them.

The big doe didn't even look my way.
She was in a zone
shamans and monks meditate for years
to achieve.
Her brand new fawn
wobbled along behind
to the other wood-side.

Before they faded
into the green undergrowth,
I pulled up beside them
and shifted into neutral.
The spotted fawn paused
and stared back at me.
Its gaze wasn't young and innocent,
but elfin and old as instinct.

It could have been my wild imagination
I saw,
or an insight
into the old spirit world
that lights up
in Paleolithic cave paintings.

My window was open.
The fawn's eyes
were dark as cavern walls
before the torches and pigments.   ■

For Blaise

Our eighteen-year-old daughter
wants to know if she's
inspired me lately.

"Yes," I answer,
"every time you drive in the driveway
safe late at night."

That's not what she wants to hear.
"I mean, have you written
any new poems about ME?"

She drives a hard bargain,
doesn't like how I exaggerate
or write things she didn't say.

She's the same age her mother was
when I met her,
and that's puzzling.

"How did you meet Mom?"
"At a dance club."
"What was your pickup line?"
"Do you want to dance
the whole next set?"

How can I tell her
she's part of the music,
and we're still dancing.   ■

Sad Birthday

Jessica was born on September 11, 1990.
The sixth-grader skipped to school
that morning hoping
to hear her name announced
over the school intercom.
It wasn't.
The terrorists' attacks
on the World Trade Center
and Pentagon;
the exploding jetliners,
and smoke and dust storms
ruined her birthday.
"It always will from now on."

Jessica always says a prayer to God
before she goes to sleep.
On her birth night she prayed
for all the "killed" people.
The girl also complained to God,
"That if He was going to let
such a bad thing happen,
why couldn't He have done it
on September 12th "?
Jessica knows
her prayer was selfish,
but she's only eleven and human.   ■

The Turcott Barn

Bill McLachlan who's eighty-three
says that when he was ten,
"The Turcott barn looked just like it does now."

Behind the barn
the cleared land
that grew beans, potatoes, milk cows,
beef cattle that were half wild,
and two generations of cherry orchards,
is being bulldozed
and reshaped with earthmovers
into a golf course
and condominiums.

In the long shadows I walk
the raw rolling landscape,
inspecting more boulders surfacing
after thousands of years.

Took time off from writing
to work with a crowbar and hammer
in the warm August shade.
I pry weathered grey boards
off the north side of the Turcott barn,
salvaging old fossil planks
before time erases the building
like it did the forests
these slabs came from.

Below the empty haymows
rusty stanchion chains lie where they dropped
when the cows left sixty years ago.
Haul two loads of lumber home.
Pull out the decayed nails
and wash the corduroyed grains
with laundry soap.
Hose away centennial dust and orchard sprays.

The wet whorls and knots
remind me of driftwood.

The ghost town men
who nailed these boards up
must've eaten lunch in the shade
with their wagons parked
and horses grazing.
Their conversations,
hammering and sawing
like everyday history
thinned into air.   ∎

The Barn Burning

Time like sunlight is a fire …
and the Torch Lake Township firemen
have come to the Turcott barn
a hundred years after it was built
to put it out.

They bring two fire trucks
and a water tank.
They snake hoses from the trucks
by the road
to the barn,
and spray the old dry boards
so they won't burn too fast,
and the picker shacks close by.

A small crowd gathers to watch,
but the firemen make us stand way back.

At 7:30 p.m.
the legal vandals light seed fires
in the southeast and southwest corners.

Orange and green flames
grow like vines
over and through the roof.
Twirling black smoke
stains the April blue sunset.

By eight o'clock nothing's left
except one burning upright beam
(that used to be a tree)
still standing on a cement foundation.
Smoldering steel roof sheets
lie in a mound of ashes.
Some starlings and grackles fly around
where their nests had been.

Bill McLachlan who's eighty-three
says when he was ten,
"The Turcott barn looked just like it did."
He mumbles something sarcastic
about progress.   ■

Spirit Dandy

Which one of my earth bodies
will I wear
in the next world
after I die?

I don't want
to promenade around
in my bare spirit.
Will I have a closet full
of my physical phases.

Where will one look end
and the next begin?

Time happening all at once
must look like cubism.

Just in case …

I've been on a diet
all morning.
Started exercising again too.
Did thirty push-ups
and thirty sit-ups
in two groups of fifteen.

I'm pumped up
and ready for a power walk
to the mailbox.

Checked myself out twice
in the mirror.
I'm looking better already.
Think I'll do some toe-touches
before lunch.   ■

Part Six

Poems From Lifelines
 A World War II Story of Survival and Love,
 Based on an Oral history of Jack and Leda Miller

This is Jack Miller's tale about experiencing the Bataan Death March, and being a prisoner of war for all of World War II. At my wife's urging, I added his wife's story about waiting for him at home. Leda's voice is in italics. T.W.

Hell's Yard

We walked to a highway
where lost American troops
were massing in retreat.
Nobody knew
what was happening.
Us lonesome soldiers walked all night
into the next morning.
There we found out
we'd been surrendered.

The Japanese made us throw our rifles down
in a pile.
They sat us in a hot field
for half a day
with enemy planes flying over.

You can't imagine
the isolation and hopelessness
of being so far from home,
thousands and thousands of miles
and out of control
of your own life
under the power
of the rising New Order
as the Japanese called themselves.

There's no feeling I've ever had
that compares.
The whole bottom of my life
seemed to drop out.
What am I doing here?
How did I end up here?
Then they herded us out.   ■

The Bataan March

We were sick
and half starved
from a low-calorie diet
before starting
the Bataan March.
They didn't call it the Death March
until so many of us died.

The hike was sixty to ninety miles
from Mariveles
to San Fernando
in 95-degree heat.
We walked on blisters,
bleeding feet,
meat to raw bone
on hot pavement.

For five days I don't remember
getting any food or water.
Anybody who fell out
was either shot
or bayoneted.
Anything that could happen
did.

Married men tore up and threw away photos
of their wives
and kids,
so Japanese guards couldn't
desecrate them.

There was a smashed out figure
of a person
like a silhouette
in the road.
He'd been run over by a tank
and left to dry in the sun.

It looked like someone had drawn
a flat picture.
Nobody in our group knew
who he was.

We spent nights
in cramped hot buildings without toilets,
or in filthy fields full of mosquitoes.

During the heat of the day
sometimes Japanese guards would stop
and make us stand still.
It was called the "sun treatment."

Filipino citizens
tried to sneak us food and water,
or they'd flash us the victory sign.

When Japanese soldiers weren't looking,
old Filipino women
with long full skirts
would motion for prisoners
to crawl under their hems
and hide
till the guards had passed.
A few escaped that way.

In San Fernando
they loaded what was left of us
on freight trains
a hundred men per boxcar.
It was so crowded you couldn't sit down
and so hot guys died.
Most of us had malaria and dysentery.
The stink was suffocating.

After unloading in Capas
we walked another ten miles
to Camp O'Donnell.

From my point of view …
I went through the whole experience
with an indifferent feeling.
I wasn't playing mental games
with myself.
I just ignored what reality was
and tried to stay
out of the way.

Years later I'd wake up all sweaty.
The dreams were always accurate
and matched reality.
The nightmares stopped
when I started talking about it.   ∎

Staring At the Cards (Leda)

I was over at Jack's folks'
playing cards
when we found out about Pearl Harbor
and Clarks and Nichols Field
in the Philippines.
It came over the radio.

I found out about the Death March
at his folks' too.
Jack's dad said I turned
white as a sheet.

I can't remember what the news said.
It was sad …
but after
a while we kept on playing cards
because what could you do?

I had my own bed
in Jack's room.
It made me feel closer to him
or worse.   ■

A Water Spigot

At Camp O'Donnell
things were pretty crude.

There were six or seven thousand prisoners
with no toilets
except trench ditches
with globs of flies.
You had to fight the flies
to go to the bathroom.

We had one water spigot
with a slow stream.
Guys used to take six or seven canteens
and take turns waiting
in line all day.

To get out of such bad conditions
some of us volunteered
for a bridge building detail.
With shovels and wheelbarrows
it took thirty days.

The food was better
if you liked as many worms as rice.
When it was over
they moved us by truck
to Camp Cabanatuan.   ■

Camp Cabanatuan

Things got tough in Camp Cabanatuan.
There was a fence around us
and barbed wire
with guard towers.
Except for the guards in the towers
the Japanese stayed in the center
and kept the prisoners around them
for protection
against snipers.

We got two little bowls of rice
with green stuff;
one in the morning
and one at night.

Between meals
a guard might come up and shoot you
for no reason.
Luck had a lot to do with surviving.
Quite a few guys got their heads cut off
with big swords.

Another favorite prison guard pastime
was making prisoners beat up on each other.
Some pretty strong characters just gave up.
At Camp Cabanatuan
thirty-five to forty guys died every day.

A lot of the dead
were buried in such shallow pits,
hungry dogs and wild animals
dug 'em up and ate 'em.

I caught malaria and dysentery
and developed ulcers in both eyes.
I couldn't tell a man from a carabao
twenty feet in front of me.   ■

Talking to Spirits (Leda)

A lot of people
were playing the Ouija board,
so Jack's younger brother
and I started playing.

There's even a family photograph of us
tucked away somewhere
playing it.

I'd ask the spirits
questions like,
if Jack was okay
and if he was coming home.

The Ouija board always answered
he would return,
that he was all right.

Course I didn't believe in those things.

Jack's brother
said he wasn't pushing it,
and I wasn't.
I don't know what
made our fingers move.

I had my palm read too.
My fortune was
that Jack was coming home.
My lifeline was
still connected to his.   ■

Sunrises and Sunsets

There were sunrises and sunsets
but we didn't admire them.

I can't think of one
beautiful thought
I had in three and a half years.

If you were going to
think about something
it was the type of food
you were going to cook,
and how you were going to get it.

Guys would talk about movies
and girls,
but the conversation would
always come back around
to food.

If you saw a song bird hopping along
you wanted to eat it.

Not even many humorous things
happened except,
this one prisoner got ahold
of some night crawlers
and boiled 'em.
He came out with solid dirt.
Cooked night crawlers are solid dirt.
You're better off
eating 'em raw.   ■

Hell Ships

On September 6, 1943,
after one and a half years
in the Philippines,
us scarecrow men
were shipped to Japan
in unmarked freighters
called "Hell Ships."
They jammed three to four hundred
men to a hold.
Food was lowered
down in buckets.
There was a toilet
up on deck over the side.
We took turns.
I was up there a few times,
but not for long
because so many of us
wanted to go.
The fresh air
sure felt good.
U.S. Navy submarines
were torpedoing
Japanese freighters
because they didn't know
we were in there.
The stinking trip
took twenty-nine days
with a layover in Formosa
for repairs.   ■

Setetsu Steel Mill

I was in a camp of four hundred prisoners
surrounded by a wooden fence
and Japan.

The prison was about a mile
from Hirohata,
a small port town
with a shipyard
where boats unloaded coal
for a steel plant.

We worked for
Setetsu Steel Mill.
I'll never forget that name.

These overhead cranes
came out on tracks
and would scoop up a big scoop
and carry it into the plant.
When they got down so far
they'd leave little piles.

My job was shoveling
the little piles of coal
into big piles.
For two years
this went on and on.

Every morning in rain, snow or sunshine
we were marched to work.
Perhaps of all the time
I was a prisoner
I got lucky,
compared to the men in the ship holds
or coal mines.   ■

Postcard of the Bomb

My old friend Bud
was in Nagasaki two days after
Japan surrendered
after we dropped the A-bombs.

He served on an aircraft carrier.
The U.S. Navy sailed up a wide river
that opened into a harbor.
A Zen poetry land of
grass, trees and houses
with no visible damage
sloped up from the blue water.

The hill had buffered the harbor
from the nuclear blast.
Nobody knew what the destruction
would look like
on the other side.
They found an old abandoned truck,
got it started,
and went sightseeing.

Nothing was left
at the center of town
except some steel wheels of a train
that had been blown away.
Two charred barber chairs
stood empty on a slab of cement.

As they drove back out of Nagasaki
burnt steel frames of buildings
were like trees after a volcano.
Anything still standing was bent
in the direction
of the explosion.

After a few miles
they approached a young Japanese woman
walking with her head down.

She heard the truck
and looked up smiling,
before she realized they were Americans.

She took off like a frightened deer.
Last they ever saw of her
she was still running
through the desolation over the hill.   ■

I Went Home (Leda)

In Traverse City
on V J Day
toilet paper was hanging
from the very tops of the buildings,
and confetti was falling.

Our friend ran a store downtown.
She wouldn't let anybody in that night,
except people she knew.
My sister and I
went in.

This store owner
had been drinking
and was waving a knife around
at imaginary Japanese.
She was mad
because Jack was still gone.

She asked me
all kinds of questions
about him.

Everybody was out on the street
partying.
It was just like those famous pictures
of downtown New York City,
the sailor kissing the girls.

All kinds of young men
in uniforms
were running around
celebrating with girls.

I didn't want any part of that,
and decided to go back home
to my apartment.   ■

Taste of Home

Woke up
in Letterman General Hospital
in San Francisco.
My bed was shaking.
It wasn't an earthquake.

There was Bev Veliquette from my hometown
with a weekend pass
for me.
He was stationed
with the Navy Construction Battalion
in Oakland.

Bev and Marie and Leda and I
had double-dated
in high school.

Marie cooked me my first home cooked meal
of mashed potatoes,
a vegetable I forgot,
and tomatoes
with fried Spam.
(Meat was being rationed.
There wasn't a lot of fresh meat.)
Plus two banana cream pies.

I stayed the afternoon
and evening with them,
and caught up on three and a half years
of gossip
and news.
They had a stack of old newspapers
from Elk Rapids.
Norm was a baby then.

They told me about Leda
and my lost four years.   ■

"It's Been a Long, Long Time"

After such a long time
it was almost like our parents
had planned our marriage.

Neither of us knew what to say.
We had to think
exactly how we wanted to word things.

That length of time apart was quite a while.
We didn't know who we were.
You forget things,
but we went on with it.

She was just as ornery and pretty
as she ever was.

We were in Chicago for three months
while I was in the hospital.   ■

A Thousand Times

It's all over
now except
for occasional nightmares.
The bad dreams
happened quite often at first.

I've been captured in my sleep
a thousand times
since the end of the war.
Only difference lately
is if I get captured
my wife and kids and grandkids are with me.

It doesn't bother me to talk about it
and I'm not bitter.
The Japanese now
are a lot different people
than they were back then.   ■

A Hero?

I don't think of myself as a hero.
Don't know what I did
that would've made me a hero.

To say I feel I was part of history …
the way I figure
if somebody brings the Bataan March up,
I can say I was there
and that's about it.

Everybody is a part
of some kind of history
somewhere along the line
because of where
you happen to be.

I'm just happy that I made it back
when so many did not.

As for the fact
that I was there,
I was sent there.
I didn't volunteer.

I might not
have made it into the military,
and got run over by a car.   ■

Terry resting during the building of the Poem Dome at Stone Circle, summer 1998.

Part Seven

Poems From Child of War
   Based on an Oral History of Hannie Kuieck

I wanted to challenge myself and show war through the eyes of a child, in this case a little girl. I found the story in a woman who had spent her first five and a half years growing up in the Netherlands under Nazi occupation. T.W.

War

There's a huge statue
by the harbor in Rotterdam,
very well known throughout the world,
it's so well done.

It's a beautiful, stunning monument
of a great big man
with a hole where his heart is.
He's looking up
and his arms are reaching to the sky
in desperation.

I don't know
where evil comes from …
but people have been invading territory
and killing different people
since time began.

The first five years of my life
were under Nazi occupation.
I thought the Nazi flag
was just colorful,
all that red and black.   ■

A Safe Place

I was just an infant
when my paps took our family inland
to Arnhem,
a small town
close to the German border.
The location didn't matter.
All the land was occupied.

Paps thought
it would be a safe place
till we knew
what was going on.

We rented a house
on the northern outskirts of Arnhem
above the Rhine
where most of the city was.
The rent was too much.
Paps said in his notes
that he could hardly pay.
We lived there four and a half years.

I can pinpoint
where my house was.
There's a road
that goes in a curve
with a park on the other side.

Arnhem turned out to be the worst place.
At the end of the war
we were right smack-dab in the middle,
in the eye of the storm
of a terrible battle
like a chess game.　　■

Eyes

My parents were hiding their feelings
and not happy.
In some of the old pictures,
even those of a normal family pose,
if you look close
at their eyes
you can tell something is wrong.

Mams covered my eyes a lot
if something bad happened,
like when the truck went by
full of bodies.

The Dutch underground had a plan
to kill one
of the main German commanders.
They didn't succeed.

The Germans didn't catch anybody.
So they went to the center of Arnhem,
picked out twenty-five young
men and boys
and just killed them …
to scare the population
into knowing this assassination attempt
could not happen again.

Their bodies were hauled by in a truck
with all their legs sticking out.
Paps told me what happened,
but I didn't see the bodies.   ■

I Heard

I was quiet
and listened to adults a lot.
I developed a firm grip
of what it's like
having your country taken
away from you.

My parents didn't bad-mouth the Germans
around me.
Words like that
coming out of a child's mouth
could've really got us in trouble,
but I overheard things.

The German soldiers were really loud
and marched around in groups
and never spoke to me.
Mams wouldn't let me go near them.

People wanted them dead.
They were not in friendly territory
and didn't feel at home,
though they acted like it.

Mams used to say,
"They act like they're going to stay,
but they're not.
They're going to get out
sooner or later."   ■

An Empty Noise

I didn't have the freedom
to be a child.
We didn't have toys and candy,
but we didn't know the difference.
I collected rocks.

I had a shoe box full
of colored pieces of melted glass
and empty bullet casings
to entertain myself with.
I built all sorts of things with empty shells,
colored glass and stones.

I used to whistle through the casings,
and sometimes I carried
them all in a sack.
They made a nice noise jingling.
My older brother wanted them,
but Mams made him leave me alone.

We didn't go out to restaurants
or anywhere.
We stayed home.
I had a little backyard
that I played in.

There was a wild poppy field
behind our house.
It wasn't blooming
and I couldn't stand it.
So I picked some.
I took the buds apart
where they're all wrinkled inside.
I made them into flowers.
I wanted them to do something
rather than just sit there.   ■

Up There

As a kid, to amuse myself,
I used to lie on my back
and look at the clouds.
They have beautiful clouds in the Netherlands.
Some of the old masters
painted them.
The clouds are just like those paintings.
They change a lot.
So I had my own entertainment
up there in the sky.

But then the Allied bombers
would fly over,
and the sirens would go off.
They were heavy, loud planes,
just like monsters up there
in the sky,
one wave after another
bombing the Germans
who were still there
and retreating.   ■

In the Wind

I figured out
a few years ago
why I'm terrified of bed sheets
drying in the wind.

There was a small insane asylum
close by
with thirty or forty people
wearing white nightgowns.

The battle was going on and they got out
and were running through the woods.
It was nighttime.
The bombings were like fireworks.
You could hear big guns
all around.

Mams was going nuts.
The scary people
would come to the window
and peek in
and pound on the glass.

They wanted to come in,
because it was terrible out there
like a horror movie.
These poor people
didn't know where to go
or where to run.

When I see white sheets
blowing …
I just get sickly. ■

Eye of the Storm

Those two nights of the battle
our house was
in such a position
our windows were broken.

We slept under the bed
with the mattress covering us.

Grenade fire
was coming out of the sky ...
it could have been shrapnel.
Bullets were flying
through the house.

I remember Paps picking some death things
off the floor.
That was the battle of *Oosterbeek*.

Fireworks don't bother me.
I concentrate on the colors.   ■

Like Dolls

I was about five.
After three days
of rain and fog,
I saw the second wave
of parachuters floating down
like mushrooms out of the sky ...
thousands and thousands of them
up in the air
and being shot.

It wasn't even a battle
because they didn't even have their guns ready.
I saw them dead.
They looked like dolls that had fallen down
lying in a field.   ■

Blondie

Allied soldiers
who must have been survivors and conquerors
camped out right by our house.
They were grubby and smiling,
I guess happy to be alive.

Australians, English, Polish and Americans ...
they'd call, "Hey, Blondie,
come here,"
because I had white hair.

I'd go right over and talk to them
with my little apron,
and they'd fill it
with chocolates and chewing gum
and stuff from their rations.

They seemed happy
always joking with the little girl.
Because my name was Hannie
they called me, "Honey."
Everybody thought that was so cute.
That's how I had my first chocolate bar.

There's nothing
like a little girl
to cheer up troops
who'd been through *donder*.

Then I'd go home and share my treats
with everybody.   ■

Wooten sharing a moment of levity while
building the fire for a Stone Circle evening, 2014.
Photo by Wendi Wooten.

Part Eight

The Elders Project

We brought elders of the communities into middle and high schools, and students interviewed them using tape recorders. Students selected their favorite story to transcribe. They turned this rough prose into a free verse poem using the elder's own words. I transcribed the rest of the tapes and wrote around the kids. These poems are a selection of my work. Many of these poems deal with World War II themes, because it was the major event of this generation. T.W.

Mary Joseph (96)
Pacifist

I was born in 1914
in Pennsylvania
at the foot of a small mountain.

1914 was the first year
of World War I.
That was a long time ago.

We moved to Michigan
when I was almost five.
I've lived here ever since.

I had cousins who took part
in that war.
I have stories
about World War I,
but don't dwell on them.
I don't believe in war.
I'm totally against war.

I remember the veterans.
One in particular
lived in Onekama on Main Street.

He was crippled
and couldn't talk quite straight,
or walk.
His hands were deformed
from the war.

He was lonely
and good natured.
When we passed along the street
We would stop to talk to him.

234

There were several other veterans
in the village.
One had his leg cut off.
That was scary for a little girl.

He was mad at the world.
Us girls kept our distance
or walked away.

Boys would taunt him,
call him, "Peg Leg,"
things like that.

If they taunted him too much,
he'd take his wooden leg off
and tell them if they didn't stop
he would beat them.

Course he only had one leg
to hop around on,
so he wasn't too dangerous.

I'm 96 years old
and have never lived through an era
when we were not involved in a war.
One of my best friends
I went to high school with
was killed in World War II.

I've always wished
we'd not have another war.
It's a strong thought in me.   ■

Evelyn Sorenson (95)
"We"

In 1927 Charles Lindbergh flew across
the Atlantic Ocean.
It was the first time
anyone had flown
across that big expanse of water.

I was twelve years old.
Lindbergh was everyone's hero
for a long time.
Referring to his accomplishments
Charles always said, "We."

A lot of artists,
when they look
at something they've created
think, "Did I do that?"

It seems something was there
besides their own limitations.

I just wrote a blues song
that was played down in Memphis
at a national blues contest.

A friend of mine was there
with his band,
and played my song.
He liked to tell everybody
that his friend who is 95
wrote it.

My main art is tapestries.
One of them won a contest
a couple months ago.

When I look at my tapestry that won
best of show,
I have that "We" feeling too.
Could I have done that myself?
There must've been some help.

I think that's what Charles Lindbergh
was talking about.   ■

Don Stewart (83)
High Bridge

If you drive down High Bridge Road
south of Brethren
headed north …
on the corner of River Road
and High Bridge,
you can see an old trail
coming through the woods
at an angle.

That's the old railroad grade
going up the east side of the hill.
If you look east from the road
about ninety feet,
that's where the bridge was.

The High Bridge
crossed the Manistee River Valley.
If you wanted to go places
you took the train.
There weren't any roads,
just trails.

One elderly lady told me
a story about that train years ago.
Riding the passenger cars
across the High Bridge
she said looking out the windows
you couldn't see the bridge.
It was like flying.

They were just kids,
and would go to the bathroom
and flush the toilet.
There was no tank under the bowl.
The water poured out on the tracks.

So they would flush the toilet
and look through the hole
at the bridge
and the river way below.   ■

Betty Dunham (81)
First Words

My tongue was attached wrong underneath
when I was born.
They used to call it tongue-tied.
I had trouble nursing
and couldn't talk well.

I learned to swear in Norwegian
before I could speak.
I would go to the barn with Grandpa
to milk cows.
If he got mad at a cow
he'd swear in Norwegian.

I was three when somebody discovered
my membrane
that attaches the tongue
to the floor of my mouth
was short.

Six months later,
the night my brother was born
the doctor came to help deliver him.

Dad grabbed ahold of me
and held me tight.
The doctor opened my mouth
and clipped that membrane.
There was blood all over.

They say I used some real bad swear words
in Norwegian.
Grandmother wasn't very happy about this.

I've had a loose tongue
ever since.   ■

Bruce McLachlan (79)
Bingo

I ran into my future wife at a bingo game
at the Town Hall.

Mother loved bingo,
and Dad worked all the time.
She'd go anyplace,
but wouldn't drive.
You couldn't keep her at home.

Somehow we got to the Town Hall.
I was in the seventh grade,
sitting on one end of the table,
and this gal was on the other end.
We started flirting.

She was the best looking gal
I'd ever come across.
Jeez!
I couldn't concentrate
on my bingo cards.

I asked somebody,
"Who's that girl?"
"That's Lillian Miller."

She lived in town
with her parents,
who came from Torch Lake Bridge.
She started working at the drugstore
when she was eleven.

Her oldest brother, Jack,
was a in a Japanese POW camp.　■

Dick Miller (86)
Martin Marauders

I was in the Ninth Air Corps,
and flew medium-sized bombers.
B-26's were called Martin Marauders,
and had a crew of six.

We'd fly in formations of six planes,
and were assigned to flight squadrons.
That's the way we traveled.

Germans were good with those guns. (Chuckles)
I saw an awful lot of flak.
It wasn't nice,
but it didn't bother you much.
You had certain things to do
and you'd better do it right.
That kept your mind off
the exploding pieces of steel.

When you got to your target
we had what was called a "Norton Bomb Sight."
It was one of the first computers.
You'd put in wind speed,
ground distance
and plane speed.
When you saw the X you dropped.

I had to fly straight and level
for about a minute
to get the bomb site to work.
The target area
was always protected.
They were shooting the heck out of you.   ■

Dick Miller
Zig Zag

We'd bomb at 15,000 feet.
When they shot at you
from the ground
it took twenty seconds
for the shells to reach us.

Before and after bombing
we'd count fifteen seconds,

and make a turn,
maybe two turns.
The Germans tried to outguess you.

The higher you were
the safer you were.
Sometimes we'd go up to 16,000 feet
for a few minutes,
but we didn't have oxygen,
and it was cold up there.

You didn't have to worry
about German fighter planes.
They stayed away from you
because of the flak.
We saw German fighter planes around,
but never got attacked by one.

We'd drop
and get out of there.   ■

Dick Miller
Loose in London

Crews took turns
going on what we called "Flak Leave."
In the summer guys would go
down to the French Rivera.

They gave our crew a month off in England
in early spring.
For two weeks we had a hotel
on the west side of the coast.

Three officers and three enlisted men,
We had rooms and food,
beer and booze
and we could do anything we wanted.

Then they turned us loose in London
for two weeks.
I was twenty-one,
and girls were pretty back then too.

We were in Piccadilly Circus,
a theater and amusement area
on the main square in West London
when we heard the news.
The war ended in Europe
on May 8, 1945.
People went crazy.

Right about that time
we were supposed to go back
and finish our missions.
We all drank
and did things that were normal
I shouldn't talk about.
My memories are a little vague.

After a few more days
we went back to our squadron,
but we didn't have to go bombing anymore.
That was the idea
that took getting used to.
I flew twenty-eight missions.   ■

Stanley Holzhauer (84)
Iwo Jima "Beach Party"

(I)

Iwo Jima was divided up
into six beaches
about 200 miles long.

The whole coast line is rugged.
The only suitable landing area
was on the south side
at the foot of Mount Suribachi.

The beaches were color coded.
There was Green,
Red I and II,
Yellow I and II
and Blue.

The whole landing area
was about a mile long.
I landed in the sixth wave
two or three minutes after the first.

What happened
was they didn't allow for the black sand,
the volcanic ash.
It was a mess.

We couldn't get on the island.
The beach was full of boats
that were stuck.
And the Japanese were shooting at us
from both sides high up.

(II)

Iwo Jima was my first experience
with war.
It was bad;
a bloody, bloody battle.

You see a lot of death,
a lot of body parts,
a lot of pain.

It's hard to describe how you feel
about your buddy
right next to you
having his head cut open
by a shell.

One guy I was with
was from Alpena.
We were both nineteen,
and he died instantly on Iwo.

First it's horrible,
it gets overwhelming.
Soon it's, "Hey, this is real.
This is war.
We've got to go on."
You pray a lot.

We had orders to follow
and went on with our business.

I was on the beach
not quite six days,
and lost four close friends.
We were all close,
and ten or twelve of our fifty
were injured.

(III)

On the fourth day
Mount Suribachi was taken
to stop the firing from the mountain.

I witnessed the first flag raising
and the famous photo one.
We were right down underneath
200 yards away.

I didn't know any of the guys
who raised the flags.
They were 4th Marines,
Green Beach boys.
We were Red Beach.

On the fifth day
the airport was secured.
Red Beach II Marines took it.
It was their job.
At that point
our "Beach Party" group
was no longer needed.

We were taken off the beach
on a Landing Ship Tank,
transferred to a smaller boat
and back to our ship.

(IV)

The USS Hansford was emptied
of 1,000 people.

Our crew was 600,
and being an Attack Personnel Transport
we had health-care facilities,

a good medical dispensary
and doctors available.

The USS Hansford
started to receive the wounded
off the beach.

Carrying several hundred of them
we sailed off
for Saipan.
The trip took five day or six days
with several burials at sea.

(V)

They built a platform
like a huge door
hinged to the side of the ship.

The body was prepared
down in the medical area,
dressed in uniform
and put in a body bag
made of canvas material.

They loaded the bag
with a five or six-inch gun shell
so it would sink …
not float on the surface.

We stood out there on the deck
that's open.
The person was brought out
on a stretcher
draped under an American flag.

He was placed on that platform.
The chaplain read who he was,

talked a little bit of his obituary,
where he was born and raised.

There was a brief
account on how he was killed.
A gun salute
varied with different burials.
A bugler …

A couple seamen raised the platform
like a huge door.
The person slipped out
from under the flag
into the ocean.   ■

Stanley Holzhauer
Peace

We came in battle formation.

Every aircraft carrier, light cruiser,
"battle wagon," heavy "tin can"
and all the destroyer escorts
that were in the Pacific Ocean
seemed to be there.

We called destroyers "tin cans"
because they bobbled in the water,
and we called the big battleships
"battle wagons."

My ship, the USS Hansford,
was the lead flagship.
A rear admiral was aboard,
the commander of occupation forces.

The armada stopped ten miles out
at sea.

Tokyo Bay is huge,
and Yokohama is a port
inside the bay.

The whole harbor had been mined.
We told the Japanese
to do the mine sweeping.
Then we had our mine sweepers
go around.

September 2, 1945,
our thirty huge transport ships
carrying 30,000 occupational troops
all in battle gear with rifles
entered Tokyo Bay.
Nobody else had been there.

All the landing boats were ready
to go in the water,
and our soldiers prepared
to go over the side.

The Japanese kept their word
thank the Lord.

A destroyer went in
and picked up the Japanese delegation.
The Air Corps had flown in a band
of about fifteen men
to greet us at the dock.
They played "California Here I Come"
over and over again.

American personnel had been on the dock
for two days
before we steamed in.
The Air Corps blackened the sky
with airplanes.

A man we thought was Emperor Hirohito
dressed in a black suit
with a top hat and cane
stood on the back of the destroyer.
He passed right in front of our ship
in Yokohama Harbor
headed out to the USS Missouri
where the treaty was signed.

I did not see
the Peace Treaty signed.
I saw the events
that led up to it.   ■

Audrey Kaiser (81)
Halloween

I met my husband while running away
from the police.
It was Halloween
and someone was shooting streetlights out
in Ellsworth.

The police were catching anybody
running around.
I don't know how many kids
were locked up.
Irene and I and two girlfriends
hadn't done anything
but have fun.

On the outskirts of town
I crawled under a barbed wire fence,
caught my britches
and ripped a big hole in the rear end.

I tied my jacket around my waist,
and we ran across this cow pasture.

A car drove up
with a bunch of guys.
"You girls want a ride?"
We sure did.

They were two Kaiser brothers
and a friend.
All four of us girls piled into the car
and went riding around.
One of the brothers
would become my husband.

William graduated
from the old Elk Rapids high school
they tore down.
He was five years older than me,
and had been in the Army
stationed in Germany.
The war was just over. ■

Audrey Kaiser
Change

One big change that happened
during the war
was girls started wearing pants to school.
Women were working in factories
and doing men's work.
Times were changing.

My one brother was in the Navy,
and sent me a bunch of blue bell-bottoms.
I started wearing them
with white shirts and ties.

There were twelve kids in my graduating class,
eleven girls and one boy.
There had been two boys,
but one boy came to school
dressed in his mother's clothes
in retaliation of how girls were dressing.

He wore her dress,
her hat, bead-necklace
and high-heeled shoes.

He got expelled,
and enlisted in the Army.   ■

Betty Holzhauer (94)
It Was Him

My maiden name was Betty Klemm,
very German.

During World War II
I worked in a depot
serving donuts and coffee,
watching these guys
coming through from southern Illinois
to Chicago.

Stan never passed up a donut
in his life.
We probably met each other
without realizing it.

He went off to war.
I stayed home doing volunteer work
and taking care of my son.

My first husband died
of a brain tumor,
and I had a son three months later.

My first boyfriend died
on the Bataan Death March.
My second boyfriend died
in France in the war.

So I lost two boyfriends and a husband.
I was getting desperate,
and had to capture one.

In 1954 I was working as a secretary
at my son's high school.
They were having trouble
with one older teacher.

She couldn't discipline anybody,
so they brought Stanley in.

Not only did he teach,
they put him in the office with me
selling lunch tickets.
His bookkeeping was there.

I locked the door.
Stanley survived the war,
but I captured him.
Our theme song was
"It Had to Be You."
We've been married fifty-five years.   ∎

Wally Dietz (87)
Tackle With a Wooden Leg

Morris Lee had his leg cut off
in a haying accident
by one of those sickle mowers
when he was three or four.

He had a wooden leg
and didn't have much lateral movement,
so I made him a tackle.

In football practice
I'd let him carry the ball.
You could hear that wooden leg
go clickety, clickety, click.

You'd better hurry up
and get ready to tackle him,

or fall down
before he hit you.

In 1954 during the Harrison game,
Morris broke his wooden leg
in the second quarter.

I had somebody take it down
to the hardware store,
probably the store owner's brother
to fix it.

He screwed a couple metal strips
up both sides.

When he brought the leg back,
the referees
wouldn't let Morris play
until those screws
and metal strips showing
were covered with tape.

Morris' brother always stood
on the sidelines
with a tool box
during the games
in case shear pins, cords or screws
broke or came loose.   ■

Bob Blackledge (74)
In Her Arms

I used to show cattle and sheep
at different fairs.
In 1956 I was at the Cadillac fair.
Patsy Cline was singing that night.

It was the summer
between my junior and senior year.
I'd turned seventeen.

I was out in the livestock barn.
This young woman came walking
with her girlfriend
down between the animals.

She stopped and asked me
a whole bunch of questions,
and we talked about this and that.
I didn't recognize her.

She asked, "Are you
coming to the performance tonight?"
"Yes," I said,
"I like that gal singing."
She said, "Here's a couple tickets."

My seats were right up front.
When Patsy Cline came out on stage
I couldn't believe
she was the same girl
I'd talked to in the sheep barn.

Patsy hadn't recorded
"Crazy,"
"She's Got You,"
"I Fall To Pieces,"

"Walking After Midnight,"
or "Sweet Dreams" yet,
but that's how I felt.

The concert was over.
I got up and started leaving.
Pretty soon here she came
running after me.
Jeez!

"Where are you going?"
I said, "Back to the barn,
or maybe I'll walk around the midway
a little bit."
"Well," Patsy said,
"how about you and me walking
around the midway?"
Jeez!

We were together a couple hours
talking and walking.

It was late.
She asked,
"Where are you going now?"
"I sleep in the barn," I said.
Patsy suggested, "Why don't
you walk me back to my trailer."
"Fine."

Outside her trailer
she stood on the first step
so we were eye to eye.
I mentioned her great performance
she'd put on.
I got ready to leave.

Patsy threw her arms around me,
gave me a big kiss,
and said, "I'll see you next year."

I never saw her again.
She was killed in a plane crash
a few years later.

Rumor is I made out with Patsy Cline.
She doesn't deserve that.
A kiss isn't making out.
It was her way,
and that was good.

She was young.
I don't know how old.　■

Marjorie Paradis (84)
The Letter

When Martin Luther King was killed
I wrote to his wife
and told her how sorry I was.

I had lost my husband
not too long before.
My children were without a father.

I knew a little bit
what she was going through,
except my husband died naturally.

I got a nice letter back from her,
a personal one,
not a form letter.

Coretta thanked me
for letting her know
my children

were going through the same thing.
She told me she'd be all right.

I kept her letter in a box for years.
It got kind of moldy smelling.
I thought, "I'll never need that."
So I tossed it.
I threw it away just before she died.

Don't know why I did that.
I could kick myself.　　　■

Katie Sowers
Post Office Box 1 (79)

Bill Clow
was one of our best restaurant customers.
He was a very intelligent man
with a lot to offer the community.
Bill could tell you so much.
He loved our town
and knew all about it.

Bill wanted to be there for you.
He was a great man,
but he had this problem.
We had opposite experiences
with his manic depression.

Sometimes he'd walk around town
giving his money away.

We sold
candy and cigarettes at the front counter.
One day Bill came in

and stole it right in front of us.
He cleaned us out,
and took it all home.

Then of course he took his medicine
and realized what he'd done.
He brought the merchandise all back
and sincerely apologized.

Bill borrowed our phone
because he'd ripped his out of the wall
at home.
He called the telephone company
to complain
that his phone wasn't working.
The phone company wouldn't do anything,
so he ripped ours out.
You knew he wasn't right.

Extremely sensitive people
can have extreme mood swings.
We never reported him.
I loved that man.   ■

Betty Beeby (88)
Motion

I've always been fascinated
by motion.
Galileo said, "To be ignorant of motion
is to be ignorant of nature."

Every time I do a painting of cornstalks
it sells for some reason.

Cornstalks are elegant
like dancers.

There's this energy.
Why aren't we harnessing that energy,
that motion?

I've been doing a painting of water
for two years.
I put in some electrical symbols.
Now I have to take them out.
They didn't look right.

I'd say to the water,
"Stand still so I can sketch you."
Water is
the hardest motion to catch.
Dancing is much easier.

I have a bank of sweet peas
climbing on bedsprings out back.
When the pods turn dark-brown and crisp,
and the sun comes out,
if you stand and watch …
they get just warm enough
and go into a spiral
and shoot the peas far and wide.
It's incredible.

If you hold a sweet pea pod
in your hand till it warms up,
it'll go pop, pop, pop, pop!   ∎

Joani Braun (81)
Road Art

I tend to see the other side of things.
I take meanings differently.

In 2003 I was driving along
looking at the bay
thinking, "What a wonderful place to live."

Oh, my gosh,
all of a sudden …
my vision started …
I stopped to pick up
this beautiful red-winged blackbird
that had crashed into a car.

I thought, "This is incredible."
I took the dead bird home
to draw and paint
and bury.

I drive along looking at the side of the road.
When I see an animal killed by a car,
I stop and do a sketch.
If the animal isn't too heavy
I bring it home and paint its picture.

I have quite a collection
of these framed watercolors.

My children go, "Mom, why
are you painting all that blood and guts?"
I hope
people are beginning to look
and think maybe
we should be slowing down.

Maybe what I have to do yet
in art and life,
is honor these animals,
to make us more aware
of the beings living here with us …
who were here before us.   ■

Julia Pasco (90)
Epiphany

The first time I visited Stone Circle
I had an epiphany.
I can get excited about this.

The place was a lot like when
I was a child,
but the stones weren't there.
It was my father's corn field.

I got out of the car
and looked around.
It was like I was eight years old again.

I walked down that road that heads south.
As little kids
it was a footpath
through the woods
and fields.
A little creek runs
behind Stone Circle.

That's the way we used to go
to visit Uncle Will and Aunt Eva.

Will McLachlan had big workhorses.
They would see us
and get excited and run.
It was like thunder.
I was deathly afraid of them.

Seventy years later
walking down that road
I could hear those horses running.
It was an outstanding experience.　　■

About the Poet

As a Poet Bard, Terry Wooten has taken his performance poetry and writing workshop program to thousands at K-12 schools, colleges, libraries, festivals and conferences from coast to coast for the past 30 years.

He is a living anthology; weaving classic literature, ancient, contemporary and children's poetry, as well as his own work rich in humor and lore into an entertaining and educational program. His performances are variable, and can be arranged specifically for any age group.

His poems are collected in a 2015 book from Parkhurst Brothers Publishers, *"The Stone Circle Poems: The Collected Poems of Terry Wooten."* Wooten is a two-time recipient of Michigan Creative Artist Awards, as well as having been listed in the Michigan Arts and Humanities Touring Directory, and his Elders Project was awarded the 2013 State History Award in Education from the Historical Society of Michigan.

With a Great Lakes regional focus on people and places, Wooten has written poems on diverse topics that range from Ernie Harwell radio broadcasts of the Detroit Tigers baseball games to shipwrecks on the Great Lakes. He has published 10 previous books and his work has appeared in numerous publications. His book, *"Lifelines: A WWII Story of Survival and Love,"* has been turned into a play production, forensic piece, used as a book of the month selection and as the foundation for school humanities projects.

Born and raised in Osceola County, Michigan, Wooten had his imagination sparked by nature, trains, ghost towns and folklore. He attended Western Michigan University, working toward a degree in education, writing poetry on the side. In 1980 he met poet Max Ellison who taught him the magic of the oral tradition, and he has been performing his poetry and the work of over 100 other writers as a bard ever since.

The poet greets a Stone Circle audience, 2014.
Photo by Alan Newton.

Find more books and resources by American

writers and storytellers online at

www.parkhurstbrothers.com